THE PIANIST

Contents

Foreword by Andrzej Szpilman   *page* 7

1 The Hour of the Children and the Mad   11

2 War   22

3 The First Germans   33

4 My Father Bows to the Germans   42

5 Are You Jews?   51

6 Dancing in Chłodna Street   61

7 A Fine Gesture by Mrs K   75

8 An Anthill Under Threat   86

9 The *Umschlagplatz*   98

10 A Chance of Life   108

11 'Marksmen Arise!'   116

12 Majorek   126

13 Trouble and Strife Next Door   133

14 Szałas' Betrayal   141

15 In a Burning Building   151

16 Death of a City   160

17 Life for Liquor   167

18 Nocturne in C sharp minor   177

Postscript   188

Extracts from the Diary of Captain
Wilm Hosenfeld   191

Epilogue: A Bridge Between Władysław
Szpilman and Wilm Hosenfeld, by Wolf
Biermann   209

Foreword

Until a few years ago my father never spoke of his wartime experiences. Yet they had been my companions since childhood. Through this book, which I surreptitiously took from a corner of our bookshelves when I was twelve years old, I discovered why I had no paternal grandparents and why my father never talked about his family. The book revealed a part of my own identity to me. I knew he knew I had read it, but we never discussed it, and perhaps for that reason it never struck me that the book could be of any significance to other people – something pointed out by my friend Wolf Biermann when I told him my father's story.

I've lived in Germany for many years, and I am always conscious of the painful absence of communication between Jews and the Germans and Poles. I hope this book will help to close some of the wounds that are still open.

My father Władysław Szpilman is not a writer. By profession he is what they call in Poland 'a man in whom music lives': a pianist and composer who has always been an inspiring and significant figure in Polish cultural life.

My father completed his piano studies with Arthur Schnabel at the Berlin Academy of Arts, where he also studied composition with Franz Schreker. When Hitler came to power in 1933, he returned to Warsaw and began working as a pianist for Polish Radio. By 1939 he had composed scores for a number of films, as well as many lieder, chansons and songs which were very popular at the time. He played before the war with the internationally famous violinist Bronislav Gimpel, Henryk Schoering and other renowned musicians.

After 1945 he began working for Polish Radio again, and returned to concert performance as a soloist and in chamber ensembles. He wrote several symphonic works and some three hundred popular songs, many of them great hits. He also composed music for children, incidental music for radio plays, and more film scores.

He was head of the music department of Polish Radio until 1963, when he gave up the position to devote more of his time to concert tours and the Warsaw Piano Quintet founded by himself and Gimpel. After giving more than two thousand concerts and recitals all over the world, my father retired from public concert life in 1986 to devote himself entirely to composing.

It is a private regret of mine that his compositions are still almost unknown in the western world. One reason, I think, is the division of Europe into two halves culturally as well as politically after the Second World War. Throughout the world, light, entertaining music reaches far more people than 'serious' classical music, and Poland is no exception. Its people have grown up with my father's songs, for he shaped the Polish popular music scene over several decades – but the western frontier of Poland constituted a barrier to music of that kind.

My father wrote the first version of this book in 1945, I suspect for himself rather than humanity in general. It enabled him to work through his shattering wartime experiences and free his mind and emotions to continue with his life.

The book was never reprinted, although during the 1960s a number of Polish publishing firms tried to make it available for a younger generation. Their efforts were always thwarted. No explanation was given, but the real explanation was obvious: the political authorities had their reasons.

More than fifty years after its first edition, the book has now been published – a useful lesson, perhaps, to many good people in Poland, and one that may persuade them to reissue it in their own country.

Andrzej Szpilman

1 ~ The Hour of the Children and the Mad

I began my wartime career as a pianist in the Café Nowoczesna, which was in Nowolipki Street in the very heart of
the Warsaw ghetto. By the time the gates of the ghetto closed
in November 1940, my family had sold everything we could
sell long ago, even our most precious household possession,
the piano. Life, although so unimportant, had none the less
forced me to overcome my apathy and seek some way of
earning a living, and I had found one, thank God. The work
left me little time for brooding, and my awareness that the
whole family depended on what I could earn gradually
helped me to overcome my previous state of hopelessness
and despair.

My working day began in the afternoon. To get to the café
I had to make my way through a labyrinth of narrow alleys
leading far into the ghetto, or for a change, if I felt like
watching the exciting activities of the smugglers, I could skirt
the wall instead.

The afternoon was best for smuggling. The police, exhausted by a morning spent lining their own pockets, were less
alert then, busy counting up their profits. Restless figures
appeared in the windows and doorways of the blocks of flats
along the wall and then ducked into hiding again, waiting
impatiently for the rattle of a cart or the clatter of an
approaching tram. At intervals the noise on the other side
of the wall would grow louder, and as a horse-drawn cart

trotted past the agreed signal, a whistle, would be heard, and bags and packets flew over the wall. The people lying in wait would run out of the doorways, hastily snatch up the loot, retreat indoors again, and a deceptive silence, full of expectation, nervousness and secret whispering would fall over the street once more, for minutes on end. On days when the police went about their daily work more energetically you would hear the echo of shots mingling with the sound of cartwheels, and hand grenades would come over the wall instead of bags, exploding with a loud report and making the plaster crumble from the buildings.

The ghetto walls did not come right down to the road all along its length. At certain intervals there were long openings at ground level through which water flowed from the Aryan parts of the road into gutters beside the Jewish pavements. Children used these openings for smuggling. You could see small black figures hurrying towards them from all sides on little matchstick legs, their frightened eyes glancing surreptitiously to left and right. Then small black paws hauled consignments of goods through the openings – consignments that were often larger than the smugglers themselves.

Once the smuggled goods were through the children would sling them over their shoulders, stooping and staggering under the burden, veins standing out blue at their temples with the effort, mouths wide open and gasping painfully for air, as they scurried off in all directions like scared little rats.

Their work was just as risky and entailed the same danger to life and limb as that of the adult smugglers. One day when I was walking along beside the wall I saw a childish smuggling operation that seemed to have reached a successful conclusion. The Jewish child still on the far side of the wall only needed to follow his goods back through the opening. His skinny little figure was already partly in view when he suddenly began screaming, and at the same time I heard the hoarse bellowing of a German on the other side of the wall. I ran to the child to help him squeeze through as quickly as possible, but in defiance of our efforts his hips stuck in the drain. I pulled at his little arms with all my might, while his screams became increasingly desperate, and I could hear the heavy blows struck by the policeman on the other side of the wall. When I finally managed to pull the child through, he died. His spine had been shattered.

In fact the ghetto did not depend on smuggling to feed itself. Most of the sacks and packages smuggled over the wall contained donations from Poles for the very poorest of the Jews. The real, regular smuggling trade was run by such magnates as Kon and Heller; it was an easier operation, and quite safe. Bribed police guards simply turned a blind eye at agreed times, and then whole columns of carts would drive through the ghetto gate right under their noses and with their tacit agreement, carrying food, expensive liquor, the most luxurious of delicacies, tobacco straight from Greece, French fancy goods and cosmetics.

I had a good view of these smuggled goods daily in the Nowoczesna. The café was frequented by the rich, who went there hung about with gold jewellery and dripping with diamonds. To the sound of popping champagne corks, tarts with gaudy make-up offered their services to war profiteers seated at laden tables. I lost two illusions here: my beliefs in our general solidarity and in the musicality of the Jews.

No beggars were allowed outside the Nowoczesna. Fat doormen drove them away with cudgels. Rickshaws often came long distances, and the men and women who lounged in them wore expensive wool in winter, costly straw hats

and French silks in summer. Before they reached the zone
protected by the porters' cudgels they warded off the crowd
with sticks themselves, their faces distorted with anger. They
gave no alms; in their view charity simply demoralized
people. If you worked as hard as they did then you would
earn as much too: it was open to everyone to do so, and if
you didn't know how to get on in life that was your own
fault.

Once they were finally sitting at the little tables in the
roomy café, which they visited only on business, they began
complaining of the hard times and the lack of solidarity
shown by American Jews. What did they think they were
doing? People here were dying, hadn't a bite to eat. The
most appalling things were happening, but the American
press said nothing, and Jewish bankers on the other side
of the pond did nothing to make America declare war on
Germany, although they could easily have advised such a
course of action if they'd wanted to.

No one paid any attention to my music in the Nowoczesna.
The louder I played, the louder the company eating and
drinking talked, and every day my audience and I competed
to see which of us could drown out the other. On one
occasion a guest even sent a waiter over to tell me to stop
playing for a few moments, because the music made it
impossible for him to test the gold twenty-dollar coins he
had just acquired from a fellow guest. Then he knocked the
coins gently on the marble surface of the table, picked them
up in his fingertips, raised them to his ear and listened hard
to their ring – the only music in which he took any interest.
I didn't play there for long. Mercifully, I got another job in
a very different kind of café in Sienna Street, where the
Jewish intelligentsia came to hear me play. It was here that

I established my artistic reputation and made friends with whom I was to pass some pleasant but also some terrible times later. Among the regulars at the café was the painter Roman Kramsztyk, a highly gifted artist and a friend of Artur Rubinstein and Karol Szymanowski. He was working on a magnificent cycle of drawings depicting life inside the ghetto walls, not knowing that he would be murdered and most of the drawings lost.

Another guest at the Sienna Street café was one of the finest people I have ever met, Janusz Korczak. He was a man of letters who knew almost all the leading artists of the Young Poland movement. He talked about them in a fascinating way; his account was both straightforward and gripping. He was not regarded as one of the very first rank of writers, perhaps because his achievements in the field of literature had a very special character: they were stories for and about children, and notable for their great understanding of the child's mind. They were written not out of artistic ambition but straight from the heart of a born activist and educationalist. Korczak's true value was not in *what* he wrote but in the fact that he lived *as* he wrote. Years ago, at the start of his career, he had devoted every minute of his free time and every złoty he had available to the cause of children, and he was to be devoted to them until his death. He founded orphanages, organized all kinds of collections for poor children and gave talks on the radio, winning himself wide popularity (and not just among children) as the 'Old Doctor'. When the ghetto gates closed he came inside them, although he could have saved himself, and he continued his mission within the walls as adoptive father to a dozen Jewish orphans, the poorest and most abandoned children in the world. When we talked to him in Sienna Street we did not know how finely or with what radiant passion his life would end.

After four months I moved on to another café, the Sztuka (Art), in Leszno Street. It was the biggest café in the ghetto, and had artistic aspirations. Musical performances were held in its concert room. The singers there included Maria Eisenstadt, who would have been a famous name to millions now for her wonderful voice if the Germans had not later murdered her. I appeared here myself playing piano duets with Andrzej Goldfeder, and had a great success with my paraphrase of the Casanova Waltz by Ludomir Różycki, to words by Władysław Szlengel. The poet Szlengel appeared daily with Leonid Fokczański, the singer Andrzej Włast, the popular comedian 'Wacuś the Art-lover' and Pola Braunówna in the 'Live Newspaper' show, a witty chronicle of ghetto life full of sharp, risqué allusions to the Germans. Besides the concert room there was a bar where those who liked food and drink better than the arts could get fine wines and deliciously prepared *cotelettes de volaille* or *boeuf Stroganoff*. Both the concert room and the bar were nearly always full, so I earned well at this time and could just meet the needs of our family of six, although with some difficulty.

I would really have enjoyed playing in the Sztuka, since I met a great many friends there and could talk to them between performances, if it hadn't been for the thought of my return home in the evening. It cast a shadow over me all afternoon.

This was the winter of 1941 to 1942, a very hard winter in the ghetto. A sea of Jewish misery washed around the small islands of relative prosperity represented by the Jewish intelligentsia and the luxurious life of the speculators. The poor were already severely debilitated by hunger and had no protection from the cold, since they could not possibly afford fuel. They were also infested with vermin. The ghetto swarmed with vermin, and nothing could be done about it. The clothing of people you passed in the street was infested by lice, and so were the interiors of trams and shops. Lice crawled over the pavements, up stairways, and dropped from the ceilings of the public offices that had to be visited on so many different kinds of business. Lice found their way into the folds of your newspaper, into your small change; there were even lice on the crust of the loaf you had just bought. And each of these verminous creatures could carry typhus.

An epidemic broke out in the ghetto. The mortality figures for death from typhus were five thousand people every month. The chief subject of conversation among both rich and poor was typhus; the poor simply wondered when they would die of it, while the rich wondered how to get hold of Dr Weigel's vaccine and protect themselves. Dr Weigel, an outstanding bacteriologist, became the most popular figure after Hitler: good beside evil, so to speak. People said the Germans had arrested the doctor in Lemberg, but thank God had not murdered him, and indeed they almost recognized him as an honorary German. It was said they had offered him a fine laboratory and a wonderful villa with an equally wonderful car, after placing him under the wonderful supervision of the Gestapo to make sure he did not run away rather than making as much vaccine as possible for the louse-infested German army in the east. Of course, said the story, Dr Weigel had refused the villa and the car.

I don't know what the facts about him really were. I only know that he lived, thank God, and once he had told the Germans the secret of his vaccine and was no longer useful to them, by some miracle they did not finally consign him to the most wonderful of all gas chambers. In any case, thanks to his invention and German venality many Jews in Warsaw were saved from dying of typhus, if only to die another death later.

I did not have myself vaccinated. I couldn't have afforded more than a single dose of the serum – just enough for myself and not the rest of the family, and I didn't want that.

In the ghetto, there was no way of burying those who died of typhus fast enough to keep up with the mortality rate. However, the corpses could not simply be left indoors either. Consequently, an interim solution was found: the dead were stripped of their clothes – too valuable to the living to be left on them – and were put outside on the pavements wrapped in paper. They often waited there for days until Council vehicles came to collect them and take them away to mass graves in the cemetery. It was the corpses who had died of typhus, and those who died of starvation too, that made my evening journey home from the café so terrible.

I was one of the last to leave, along with the café manager, after the daily accounts had been made up and I had been paid my wages. The streets were dark and almost empty. I would switch on my torch and keep a look-out for corpses so as not to fall over them. The cold January wind blew in my face or drove me on, rustling the paper in which the dead were wrapped, lifting it to expose naked, withered shins, sunken bellies, faces with teeth bared and eyes staring into nothing.

I was not as familiar with the dead as I would become later. I hurried down the streets in fear and disgust, to get home as quickly as possible. Mother would be waiting for me with a bowl of spirits and a pair of pincers. She cared for the family's health during this dangerous epidemic as

best she could, and she would not let us through the hall
and on into the flat until she had conscientiously removed
the lice from our hats, coats and suits with the pincers and
drowned them in spirits.

In the spring, when I had become more friendly with
Roman Kramsztyk, I often did not go straight home from
the café but to his home, a flat in Elektoralna Street where
we would meet and talk until late into the night. Kramsztyk
was a very lucky man: he had a tiny room with a sloping
ceiling all to himself on the top floor of a block. Here he
had assembled all his treasures that had escaped being plundered by the Germans: a wide couch covered with a kelim,
two valuable old chairs, a charming little Renaissance chest
of drawers, a Persian rug, some old weapons, a few paintings
and all kinds of small objects he had collected over the years
in different parts of Europe, each of them a little work of
art in itself and a feast for the eyes. It was good to sit in this
small room by the soft yellow light of a lamp, with a shade
made by Roman, drinking black coffee and talking cheerfully. Before darkness fell we would go out on the balcony
to get a breath of air; it was purer up here than in the dusty,
stifling streets. Curfew was approaching. People had gone
inside and closed the doors; the spring sun, sinking low, cast
a pink glow over the zinc rooftops, flocks of white pigeons
flew through the blue sky and the scent of lilac made its way
over the walls from the nearby Ogród Saski (Saxon Garden),
reaching us here in the quarter of the damned.

This was the hour of the children and the mad. Roman
and I would already be looking down Elektoralna Street for
the 'lady with the feathers', as we called our madwoman.
Her appearance was unusual. Her cheeks were brightly
rouged and her eyebrows, a centimetre thick, had been

drawn in from temple to temple with a kohl pencil. She wore an old fringed green velvet curtain over her ragged black dress, and a huge mauve ostrich feather rose straight into the air from her straw hat, swaying gently in time with her rapid, unsteady steps. As she walked she kept stopping passers-by with a polite smile and asking after her husband, murdered by the Germans before her eyes.

'Excuse me . . . have you by any chance seen Izaak Szerman? A tall, handsome man with a little grey beard?' Then she would look intently at the face of the person she had stopped, and on receiving an answer in the negative she would cry, 'No?' in disappointment. Her face would distort painfully for a moment, but was then immediately softened by a courteous if artificial smile.

'Oh, do forgive me!' she would say, and walk on, shaking her head, half sorry to have taken up someone's time, half amazed that he had not known her husband Izaak, such a handsome and delightful man.

It was around this time of day that the man called Rubinstein also used to make his way down Elektoralna Street, ragged and dishevelled, his clothes fluttering in all directions. He brandished a stick, he hopped and jumped, he hummed and murmured to himself. He was very popular in the ghetto. You could tell he was coming quite a long way off when you heard his inevitable cry of, 'Keep your pecker up, my boy!' His aim was to keep people's spirits up by making them laugh. His jokes and comic remarks went all around the ghetto, spreading cheerfulness. One of his specialities was to approach the German guards, hopping about and making faces, and call them names – 'You scallywags, you bandits, you thieving bunch!' and all kinds of more obscene terms. The Germans thought this hilarious, and often threw Rubinstein cigarettes and a few coins for his insults; after all, one couldn't take such a madman seriously.

I was not so sure as the Germans about that, and to this day I don't know if Rubinstein was really one of the many who had lost their minds because of the torments they had suffered, or was simply playing the fool to escape death. Not that he succeeded there.

The mad took no notice of curfew time; it meant nothing to them, or to the children either. These ghosts of children now emerged from the basements, alleys and doorways where they slept, spurred on by the hope that they might yet arouse pity in human hearts at this last hour of the day. They stood by lamp-posts, by the walls of buildings and in the road, heads raised, monotonously whimpering that they were hungry. The more musical of them sang. In thin, weak little voices they sang the ballad of the young soldier wounded in battle; abandoned by all on the battlefield, he cries out, 'Mother!' as he dies. But his mother is not there, she is far away, unaware that her son lies dying, and only the earth rocks the poor man into eternal slumber with its rustling trees and grasses: 'Sleep well, my son, sleep well, my dear!' A blossom fallen from a tree to lie on his dead breast is his only cross of honour.

Other children tried appealing to people's consciences, pleading with them. 'We are so very, very hungry. We haven't eaten anything for ages. Give us a little bit of bread, or if you don't have any bread then a potato or an onion, just to keep us alive till morning.'

But hardly anyone had that onion, and if he did he could not find it in his heart to give it away, for the war had turned his heart to stone.

2 ~ War

By 31 August 1939 everyone in Warsaw had been sure for some time that war with the Germans was inevitable. Only incorrigible optimists had still cherished the delusion that Poland's determined stance would deter Hitler at the last moment. Other people's optimism manifested itself, perhaps subconsciously, as opportunism: an inherent belief, in defiance of all logic, that although war was bound to come – that had been decided long ago – its actual outbreak would be delayed, so they could live life to the full a little longer. After all, life was good.

A scrupulous blackout was imposed on the city at night. People sealed the rooms they were planning to use as gas shelters and tried on their gas masks. Gas was feared more than anything else.

Meanwhile, bands still played behind the darkened windows of cafés and bars where the customers drank, danced and stirred up their patriotic feelings by singing belligerent songs. The need for a blackout, the chance to walk about with a gas mask slung over your shoulder, a journey home at night by taxi through streets that suddenly looked different added a certain spice to life, especially as there was no real danger yet.

The ghetto had not yet been created, and I was living with my parents, my sisters and my brother in Śliska Street, working for Polish Radio as a pianist. I was late home that

last day of August, and as I felt tired I went straight to bed.
Our flat was on the third floor, a location which had its
advantages: on summer nights the dust and the street smells
subsided and refreshing air came in through our open
windows from above, carrying the moisture that rose from
the river Vistula.

The noise of explosions woke me. It was light already. I
looked at the time: six o'clock. The explosions were not
particularly loud, and seemed to be some way off: outside
the city, anyway. Obviously military exercises were in progress; we had become accustomed to them over the last
couple of days. After a few minutes the explosions stopped.
I wondered whether to go back to sleep, but it was too light
and sunny now. I decided to read until breakfast time.

It must have been at least eight when my bedroom door
opened. Mother stood there, dressed as if she was off into
town any minute. She was paler than usual, and could not
conceal a certain disapproval when she saw me still in bed
reading. She opened her mouth, but at the very first word
her voice failed her and she had to clear her throat. Then
she said, in nervous, hurried tones, 'Get up! The war . . . the
war's begun.'

I decided to go straight to the radio station, where I would
find my friends and hear the latest news. I dressed, ate breakfast and left the house.

You could already see large white posters on the walls of
buildings and the advertising pillars: they bore the president's
message to the nation announcing that the Germans had
attacked. Some people were standing around in small groups
reading it, while others hurried off in various different directions to deal with their most urgent business. The pro-
prietress of the corner shop not far from our building was

sticking strips of white paper over the windows, hoping that would keep them intact in the coming bombardment. Meanwhile, her daughter was decorating platters of egg salad, ham and sausage rings with small national flags and portraits of Polish dignitaries. Paper-boys selling special editions ran breathlessly down the streets.

There was no panic. The mood swung between curiosity – what would happen next? – and surprise: was this the way it all began?

A grey-haired, clean-shaven gentleman stood rooted to the spot beside one of the pillars bearing the presidential announcement. His agitation was visible in the bright red blotches covering his face and neck, and he had pushed his hat back on his head, something he would surely never have done in normal circumstances. He studied the announcement, shook his head incredulously and read on, pushing his pince-nez down more firmly over his nose. He read a few words out loud, indignantly. 'They attacked us ... without warning!'

He looked round at his neighbours to see their reaction, raised a hand, readjusted his pince-nez and remarked, 'Really, this is no way to behave!' And as he walked away, having read the whole thing through once more and still unable to control his agitation, he was shaking his head and muttering, 'No, no, this won't do!'

I lived quite close to the broadcasting centre, but it was not at all easy to get there; the walk took twice as long as usual. I was about halfway when the howl of sirens sounded from the loudspeakers installed on lamp-posts, in windows and over shop doorways. Then I heard the radio announcer's voice. 'This is an alarm warning for the city of Warsaw ... Be on the alert! Now on their way are ...' At this point the

announcer read out a list of figures and letters of the alphabet
in military cipher that fell on civilian ears like a mysterious
cabbalistic threat. Did the figures mean the number of aircraft on their way? Were the letters code for the places where
bombs were about to be dropped? And was the place where
we were now standing one of them?

The street rapidly emptied. Women scurried to the shelters
in alarm. The men did not want to go down; they stood in
doorways, cursing the Germans, making a great show of their
courage and venting their anger with the government for
bungling mobilization so that only a small number of the
men fit for military service were called up. The rest were
going from one military authority to another, unable to get
themselves into the army for love or money.

There was nothing to be heard in the empty, lifeless street
but the arguments between the air-raid wardens and people
who insisted on leaving the doorways of houses on some
kind of business and were trying to go on their way, keeping
close to the walls. A moment later there were more
explosions, but still not too close.

I reached the broadcasting centre just as the alarm went off
for the third time. However, no one inside the building had
time to make for the air-raid shelters whenever it sounded.

The broadcasting schedule was in chaos. As soon as something like a provisional programme had been hastily cobbled
together important announcements would come in, either
from the front or of a diplomatic nature. Everything had to
be interrupted to broadcast this sort of news as quickly as
possible, and it was interspersed with military marches and
patriotic anthems.

There was also hopeless confusion in the corridors of the
centre, where a mood of belligerent self-confidence prevailed.

One of the broadcasters who had been called up came in to say goodbye to his colleagues and show off his uniform. He had probably expected everyone to surround him for a touching and uplifting farewell scene, but he was disappointed: no one had time to pay him much attention. There he stood, buttonholing his colleagues as they hurried past and trying to get at least a part of his programme entitled 'A Civilian's Farewell' on the air, so that he could tell his grandchildren about it some day. He was not to know that two weeks later they would still have no time for him – not even time to honour his memory with a proper funeral.

Outside the studio door an old pianist who worked at the radio station took my arm. Dear old Professor Ursztein. Whereas other people measure out their lives by days and hours, his had been measured for decades by piano accompaniments. When the professor was trying to remember details of some past event, he would begin, 'Now let's see. I was accompanying so-and-so at the time . . .' and once he had pinpointed a particular accompaniment by its date, like a milestone at the road-side, he let his memory range on over other and invariably less important reminiscences. Now he stood stunned and disorientated outside the studio. How was this war to be waged without piano accompaniment – what would it be like?

At a loss, he began complaining, 'They won't tell me if I'm to work today . . .'

By that afternoon we were both working, each at his own piano. Music broadcasts were still going on, although not to the usual schedule.

In the middle of the day some of us felt hungry and left the broadcasting centre for a bite of lunch in a nearby restaurant. The streets looked almost normal. There was a great deal of traffic in the main thoroughfares of the city – trams, cars and pedestrians; the shops were open, and since the mayor had appealed to the population not to hoard food, assuring us that there was no need to do so, there were not even any queues outside them. Street traders were doing good business selling a paper toy which represented a pig, but if you put the paper together and unfolded it in a certain way it turned into Hitler's face.

We got a table in the restaurant, though with some difficulty, and it turned out that several of the standard dishes on the menu were not available today and others were rather more expensive than usual. The speculators were already at work.

Conversation revolved mainly around the forthcoming declaration of war by France and Britain that was expected very soon. Most of us, apart from a few hopeless pessimists, were convinced they would enter the war any moment now, and a number of us thought the United States would declare war on Germany too. Arguments were drawn from the experiences of the Great War, and there was a general feeling that the sole purpose of that conflict had been to show us how to conduct the present one better, and do it properly this time.

The declaration of war by France and Great Britain became a reality on 3 September.

I was still at home, although it was already eleven o'clock. We left the radio on all day so as not to miss a word of the all-important news. The communiqués from the front were not what we had expected. Our cavalry had attacked East Prussia and our aircraft were bombarding German military objectives, but meanwhile the superior military power of the enemy kept forcing the Polish army to withdraw from somewhere or other. How could such a thing be possible when our propaganda had told us that German aircraft and tanks were made of cardboard, and ran on synthetic fuel that wasn't even fit for cigarette lighters? Several German planes had already been shot down over Warsaw, and eyewitness accounts claimed to have seen the corpses of enemy airmen wearing paper clothes and paper shoes. How could such wretchedly equipped troops force us to retreat? It made no sense.

Mother was bustling about the living room, Father was practising his violin and I was sitting in an armchair reading, when some inconsequential programme was suddenly interrupted and a voice said that an announcement of the utmost importance was about to be made. Father and I hurried over to the radio set while Mother went into the next room to call my two sisters and my brother. Meanwhile the radio was playing military marches. The announcer repeated his remarks, there were more marches and yet another announcement of the forthcoming announcement. We could hardly stand the nervous tension when the national anthem was finally played, followed by the national anthem of Great Britain. Then we learned that we no longer faced our enemy alone; we had a powerful ally and the war was certain to be won, although there would be ups and downs, and our situation might not be too good for the time being.

It is difficult to describe the emotion we felt as we listened to that radio announcement. Mother had tears in her eyes, Father was sobbing unashamedly and my brother Henryk took his chance to aim a punch at me and say, quite crossly, 'There you are! I told you so, didn't I?'

Regina did not like to see us quarrelling at such a moment and intervened, saying calmly, 'Oh, do stop it! We all knew this was bound to happen.' She paused, and added, 'It's the logical outcome of the treaties.'

Regina was a lawyer and an authority on such subjects, so it was no use arguing with her.

Meanwhile, Halina was sitting by the radio set trying to tune in to London; she wanted first-hand confirmation of the news.

My two sisters were the most level-headed members of the family. Who did they take after? If anyone, it must have been Mother, but even she seemed an emotional character compared to Regina and Halina.

Four hours later France declared war on Germany. That afternoon Father insisted on joining the demonstration outside the British Embassy building. Mother was not happy about it, but he was set on going. He came back in a state of high excitement, dishevelled from the crush of the crowd. He had seen our foreign minister and the British and French ambassadors, he had cheered and sung along with everyone else, but then suddenly the crowd was asked to disperse as quickly as possible because there might be an air raid. The crowd energetically did as it was told, and Father could have been suffocated. All the same, he was very happy and in good spirits.

Unfortunately, our joy was of short duration. The communiqués from the front became more and more alarming. On 7 September, just before dawn, there was a loud knocking at the door of our flat. Our neighbour from the flat opposite, a doctor, was standing outside in high army boots, a hunting jacket and a sporting cap, carrying a rucksack. He was in a hurry, but he thought it his duty to let us know the Germans were advancing on Warsaw, the government had moved to Lublin, and all able-bodied men were to leave the city and go to the far side of the river Vistula, where a new line of defence would be built up.

At first none of us believed him. I decided to try getting information from some of the other neighbours. Henryk switched the radio on, but there was silence: the station had gone off the air.

I could not find many of our neighbours. A number of flats were locked up, and in others women were packing for their husbands or brothers, weeping and prepared for the worst. There could be no doubt that the doctor had spoken the truth.

I quickly made up my mind to stay. There was no point in wandering around outside the city; if I was going to die I would sooner die at home. And, after all, I thought, someone needed to look after my mother and sisters if Father and Henryk went. However, when we all discussed it, I found that they too had decided to stay.

Mother's sense of duty made her try to persuade us to leave the city, all the same. She looked from one to another of us, her eyes wide with fear, putting forward new arguments in favour of getting out of Warsaw. When we insisted on staying, however, instinctive relief and satisfaction showed in her fine, expressive eyes: whatever happened, it was better to be together.

I waited until eight o'clock and then went out, only to find the city unrecognizable. How could its appearance have changed so much, so completely, in just a few hours?

All the shops were closed. There were no trams on the streets, only cars, crammed full and driving fast, all going the same way – towards the bridges over the Vistula. A detachment of soldiers was marching down Marszałkowska Street. They bore themselves defiantly, and they were singing, but you could see that discipline was unusually lax: their caps were all worn at different angles, they carried their carbines just as they liked and they were not marching in time. Something in their faces suggested that they were off to fight on their own initiative, so to speak, and had long since ceased to be part of such a precise, perfectly functioning machine as the army.

Two young women on the pavement threw them pink asters, calling something out hysterically over and over again. No one paid any attention. People were hurrying along, and it was obvious that they all meant to cross the Vistula and had just a few last important things they were anxious to get done before the Germans began to attack.

These people all looked different from the evening before too. Warsaw was such an elegant city! What had become of all the ladies and gentlemen dressed as if they came straight out of a fashion magazine? The people scurrying in all directions today looked as if they were in fancy dress as hunters and tourists. They wore high boots, ski boots, ski trousers, breeches, headscarves, and they carried bundles, rucksacks and walking sticks. They had taken no trouble to make themselves look civilized as they had dressed carelessly and in obvious haste.

The streets, so clean only yesterday, were now full of rubbish and dirt. Other soldiers were sitting or lying down in side streets, on the pavement, on the kerb, in the roadway: they had come straight from the front, and their faces, bearing and gestures showed extreme exhaustion and discouragement. In fact they tried to emphasize their discouragement, so bystanders would know that the reason they were here and not at the front was because there was no point in being at the front. It was not worthwhile. Small groups of people passed on what news of the battle areas they had gleaned from the soldiers. It was all bad.

I instinctively looked round for the loudspeakers. Perhaps they had been moved? No, they were still in place, but they had fallen silent.

I hurried off to the broadcasting centre. Why were there no announcements? Why was no one trying to give heart to people and stop this mass exodus? But the place had closed down. Its management had left the city, and only the cashiers were left, hastily paying the radio station's employees and performing artists three months' salary in lieu of notice.

'What are we supposed to do now?' I caught hold of a senior administrator's hand.

He looked at me blankly, and then I saw scorn in his eyes which gave way to anger as he shook his hand free of mine.

'Who cares?' he shouted, shrugging his shoulders and striding out into the street. He slammed the door furiously behind him.

This was unbearable.

No one could persuade all these people not to flee. The loudspeakers on the lamp-posts had fallen silent, and no one cleaned the dirt from the streets. Dirt, or panic? Or the shame of fleeing down those streets instead of fighting?

The dignity the city had suddenly lost could not be restored. *That* was defeat.

Very downhearted, I went home.

On the evening of the next day the first shell from the German artillery hit the timber yard opposite our house. The windows of the corner shop, so carefully sealed with strips of white paper, were the first to fall out.

3 ~ The First Germans

Over the next few days, mercifully, the situation improved a good deal. The city was declared a fortress and given a commandant, who issued an appeal to the population to stay where they were and show themselves ready to defend Warsaw. A counter-attack by Polish troops was being organized on the other side of the bend in the river, and meanwhile we had to hold back the main force of the enemy in Warsaw until our own men came to relieve us. The situation all round Warsaw was improving too; the German artillery had stopped shelling the city.

On the other hand, enemy air raids were being stepped up. No air-raid warnings were given now; they had crippled the city and its defence preparations for too long. Almost hourly, the silver shapes of bombers appeared high above us in the extraordinarily blue sky of that autumn, and we saw the puffs of white from anti-aircraft shells fired at them by our own artillery. Then we had to hurry down into the shelters. It was no joke now: the entire city was being bombed. The floors and walls of the air-raid shelters shook, and if a bomb fell on the building beneath which you were hiding, it meant certain death: the bullet in this deadly game of Russian roulette. Ambulances were always driving through the city, and when they ran out they were supplemented by cabs and even ordinary horse-drawn vehicles, carrying the dead and injured taken from the ruins.

Morale among the population was high, and enthusiasm grew hour by hour. We were no longer relying on luck and individual initiative, as on 7 September. Now we were an army with commanders and ammunition; we had a purpose – self-defence – and its success or failure depended on ourselves. We had only to exert all our strength.

The general in command called on the people to dig trenches round the city to prevent the advance of German tanks. We all volunteered to dig: only Mother stayed at home in the morning to look after our flat and cook us a meal.

We were digging along the side of a hill on the outskirts of the suburbs. An attractive residential quarter of villas stood behind us and a municipal park full of trees in front of us. It would actually have been quite pleasant work if it hadn't been for the bombs aimed at us. They were not particularly accurate, and fell some distance away, but it was uncomfortable to hear them whistling past as we worked down in our trench, knowing that one of them might yet hit us.

On the first day an old Jew in kaftan and yarmulka was shovelling soil beside me. He dug with Biblical fervour, flinging himself on his spade as if it were a mortal enemy, foaming at the mouth, his pale face streaming with sweat, his whole body shaking, his muscles contracting. He ground his teeth as he worked, a black whirlwind of kaftan and beard. His dogged labour, far beyond his normal capacities, produced vanishingly small results. The point of his spade could hardly penetrate the baked mud, and the dry yellow clods he prised out slipped back into the trench before the poor man, making a superhuman effort, could swing his spade back and dump the mud outside the trench. Every few moments he leaned back against the wall of earth, racked with coughing. Pale as a dying man, he sipped the peppermint brew made to refresh the workers by old women who were too weak to dig but wanted to make themselves useful somehow.

'You're overdoing it,' I told him during one of his rests. 'You really shouldn't be digging when you're not strong enough.' Feeling sorry for him, I tried to persuade him to give up. He was obviously unfit for the work. 'Look, no one's asking you to do this, after all.'

He glanced at me, still breathing heavily, and then looked up at the sky, a calm sapphire blue where the little white clouds left by shrapnel still hovered, and an expression of rapture came into his eyes, as if he saw Yahweh in all his majesty there in the heavens.

'I have a shop!' he whispered.

He sighed even more deeply, and a sob burst from him. Desperation showed on his face as he fell on his spade again, quite beside himself with the effort.

I stopped digging after two days. I had heard that the radio station was broadcasting again under a new director, Edmund Rudnicki, who used to be head of the music department. He had not fled like the others, but had reassembled his scattered colleagues and opened up the station. I came to the conclusion that I would be more useful there than digging, which was true: I played a great deal, both as soloist and accompanist.

Meanwhile, conditions in the city began to deteriorate in reverse proportion, you might say, to the increasing courage and determination of its people.

The German artillery began shelling Warsaw again, first the suburbs, then the city centre too. More and more buildings lost their window panes, there were round holes in the walls where they suffered a hit, and corners of masonry were knocked off. By night the sky was red with the glow of firelight and the air full of the smell of burning. Provisions were running low. This was the one point on which the heroic city mayor Starzyński had been wrong: he should not have advised the people against laying in stocks of food. The city now had to feed not only itself but also the soldiers trapped inside it, and the Poznań army from the west that had made its way through to Warsaw to reinforce the defence.

Around 20 September our whole family moved from the Śliska Street flat to friends who lived in a flat on the first floor of a house in Pańska Street. None of us liked the air-raid shelters. You could hardly breathe the stuffy air down in the cellar, and the low ceiling seemed about to fall in any moment, burying everything underneath it with the ruins of a multi-storey building on top. But it was hard to hold out in our third-floor flat. We kept hearing shells whistle past the windows, which had lost all their glass, and one of the shells could easily hit our building on its way through the air. We decided that the first floor would be better: the shells would hit the higher storeys and explode there, and we would not have to go down to the cellar. There were already a number of people staying in our friends' flat. It was crowded, and we had to sleep on the floor.

Meanwhile the siege of Warsaw, the first chapter in the city's tragic story, was coming to an end.

It was more and more difficult for me to reach the broadcasting centre. The corpses of people and horses killed by shrapnel lay about the streets, whole areas of the city were in flames, and now that the municipal waterworks had been damaged by artillery and bombs no attempt could be made to extinguish the fires. Playing in the studio was dangerous too. The German artillery was shelling all the most important places in the city, and as soon as a broadcaster began announcing a programme German batteries opened fire on the broadcasting centre.

During this penultimate stage of the siege the population's hysterical fear of sabotage reached its height. Anyone could be accused of spying and shot at any moment, before he had time to explain himself.

An elderly spinster, a music teacher, lived on the fourth floor of the building into which we had moved to stay with our friends. It was her bad luck to bear the surname of Hoffer and to be courageous. Her courage could just as well have been described as eccentricity. No air raids or shelling could induce her to go down to the shelter instead of doing her daily two hours of piano practice before lunch. She kept some birds in a cage on her balcony and fed them three times a day with the same dogged regularity. This way of life looked distinctly odd in the besieged city of Warsaw. It seemed highly suspicious to the maids in the building. They met at the caretaker's for political conversations. After much to-ing and fro-ing they came to the firm conclusion that a teacher with so unmistakably German a name must be German herself, and her piano-playing was a secret code through which she sent signals to the Luftwaffe pilots telling them where to drop their bombs. In no time at all the excited women had made their way into the eccentric old lady's flat, tied her up, taken her downstairs and shut her in one of the cellars, along with the birds as evidence of her sabotage. Without meaning to, they saved her life: a few hours later a shell hit her flat and destroyed it completely.

I played in front of the microphone for the last time on 23 September. I have no idea myself how I reached the broadcasting centre that day. I ran from the entrance of one building to the entrance of another, I hid, and then ran out into the street again when I thought I no longer heard the whistle of shells close by. I met Mayor Starzyński at the door of the broadcasting centre. He was dishevelled and unshaven, and his face wore an expression of deathly weariness. He hadn't slept for days. He was the heart and soul of the defence, the real hero of the city. The entire responsibility for the fate of Warsaw rested on his shoulders. He was everywhere: he went along the trenches, he was in charge of the building of barricades, the organization of hospitals, the fair distribution of what little food there was, the air-raid defences, the fire services, and still he found time to address the population daily. Everyone waited eagerly for his speeches and drew courage from them: there was no reason for anyone to lose heart as long as the mayor had no doubts. Anyway, the situation did not seem too bad. The French had broken through the Siegfried Line, Hamburg had been badly bombed by the British air force and the British army might land in Germany any moment now. Or so we thought.

On that final day at the radio station, I was giving a Chopin recital. It was the last live music broadcast from Warsaw. Shells were exploding close to the broadcasting centre all the time I played, and buildings were burning very close to us. I could scarcely hear the sound of my own piano through the noise. After the recital I had to wait two hours before the shelling died down enough for me to get home. My parents, brother and sisters had thought I must be dead, and welcomed me like a man risen from the grave. Our maid was the only person who thought all the anxiety had been unnecessary. 'After all, he had his papers in his pocket,' she pointed out. 'If he'd been dead, they'd have known where to take him.'

The same day, at three-fifteen in the afternoon, Warsaw Radio went off the air. A recording of Rachmaninov's Piano Concerto in C minor was being broadcast, and just as the second, beautiful, peaceful movement was coming to an end a German bomb destroyed the power station. The loud-speakers fell silent all over the city. Towards evening, in spite of the artillery fire now raging again, I tried to work on the composition of my concertino for piano and orchestra. I kept at work on it all through September, although I found it more and more difficult to do so.

When darkness fell that evening, I put my head out of the window. The street, red with the glow of fires, was empty, and there was no sound but the echo of bursting shells. To the left, Marszałkowska Street was burning, and so were Królewska Street and Grzybowski Square behind us and Sienna Street straight ahead. Heavy blood-red masses of smoke loomed above the buildings. The roadways and pave-ments were sprinkled with white German leaflets; no one picked them up, because they were said to be poisoned. Two bodies lay under a street-lamp at the crossroads, one with arms spread wide, the other curled up as if to sleep. Outside the door of our building lay the corpse of a woman with her head and one arm blown off. A bucket lay tipped over beside her; she had been fetching water from the well. Her blood flowed into the gutter in a long, dark stream, and then ran on into a drain covered by a grating.

A horse-drawn cab was progressing with some difficulty down the road, coming from Wielka Street and making for Żelazna Street. It was difficult to see how it had got here, and why horse and driver seemed as calm as if nothing were going on around them. The man stopped his horse on the corner of Sosnowa Street, as if wondering whether to turn off there or drive straight on. After brief reflection he chose to go straight ahead; he clicked his tongue, and the horse trotted on. They were about ten paces away from the corner when there was a whistling sound, a roar, and the street lit up with white light for a moment, as if in a flashlight photograph – I was dazzled. When my eyes were used to the twilight again, there was no cab left. Splintered wood, the remains of wheels and shafts, bits of upholstery and the shattered bodies of driver and horse lay by the walls of the buildings. If he had turned down Sosnowa Street instead . . .

The dreadful days of 25 and 26 September came. The noise of explosions merged with the constant thunder of guns, penetrated by the boom of nose-diving aircraft like electric drills boring holes in iron. The air was heavy with smoke and the dust of crumbling bricks and plaster. It got everywhere, stifling people who had shut themselves up in cellars or their flats, keeping as far as possible from the street.

How I survived those two days I do not know. A splinter of shrapnel killed someone sitting next to me in our friends' bedroom. I spent two nights and a day with ten people standing in a tiny lavatory. A few weeks later, when we wondered how it had been possible, and tried to squeeze ourselves in there again, we found that only eight people could possibly fit in unless they were in terror for their lives.

Warsaw surrendered on Wednesday, 27 September.

It was two more days before I dared to go out into the city. I came home in a deep depression: the city no longer existed – or so I thought at the time, in my inexperience.

Nowy Świat was a narrow alley winding its way through heaps of rubble. At every corner I had to make detours round barricades constructed from overturned trams and torn-up paving slabs. Decaying bodies were piled up in the streets.

The people, starving from the siege, fell on the bodies of horses lying around. The ruins of many buildings were still smouldering.

I was in the Aleje Jerozolimskie when a motor-bike approached from the direction of the Vistula. Two soldiers in unfamiliar green uniforms and steel helmets were sitting on it. They had large, impassive faces and pale blue eyes. They stopped beside the pavement and called to a startled boy. He went over to them.

'Marschallstrasse! Marschallstrasse!'

They kept repeating that one word – the German for Marszałkowska Street. The boy simply stood there, baffled, with his mouth open, unable to utter a sound.

The soldiers lost patience. 'Oh, the hell with it!' shouted the driver, making an angry gesture. He stepped on the gas and the bike roared away.

Those were the first Germans I saw.

A few days later bilingual proclamations went up on the walls of Warsaw, issued by the German commandant and promising the population peaceful working conditions and the care of the German state. There was a special section devoted to the Jews: they were guaranteed all their rights, the inviolability of their property, and that their lives would be absolutely secure.

4 ~ My Father Bows to the Germans

We went back to Śliska Street. We found our flat unharmed, although we had thought it impossible; some window panes were missing, but nothing else. The doors had been locked, and even the smallest objects were still in their old places inside the flat. Other houses in the area had also remained unharmed or had suffered only minor damage. Over the next few days, when we began going out to see what had become of our acquaintances, we discovered that, badly damaged as the city had been, in essence it was still standing. The losses were not as heavy as you might have thought at first, walking through the great expanses of ruins that were still smoking.

The same was true of the people. Initially there was talk of a hundred thousand dead, a figure which amounted to almost 10 per cent of the population of the city and horrified everyone. Later we discovered that about twenty thousand people had died.

They included friends whom we had seen alive only a few days before, and who now lay under the ruins or smashed to pieces by shells. Two of my sister Regina's colleagues had died when a building collapsed in Koszykova Street. Passing that building, you had to hold a handkerchief to your nose: the nauseating stink of eight rotting bodies seeped through the blocked-up cellar windows, through nooks and crannies, infecting the air. A shell had killed one of my own colleagues in Mazowiecka Street. Only after his head was found was it possible to establish that the scattered remains belonged to a human being who had once been a talented violinist.

Dreadful as all this news was, it could not disturb our animal pleasure in still being alive ourselves, and knowing that those who had escaped death were no longer in any immediate danger, although the subconscious mind repressed these feelings out of shame. In this new world, where everything that had been of permanent value a month ago was destroyed, the simplest things, things you hardly noticed before, took on enormous significance: a comfortable, solid armchair, the soothing look of a white-tiled stove on which you could rest your eyes, the creak of the floorboards – a comfortable prelude to the atmosphere of peace and quiet at home.

Father was the first to take up his music again. He escaped reality by playing his violin for hours on end. When someone interrupted him with a piece of bad news, he would listen and frown, looking irritated, but his face soon cleared again, and he would say, raising his violin to his chin, 'Oh, never mind. The Allies are sure to be here in a month.' This stock answer to all the questions and problems of the time was his way of closing the door behind him and returning to that other world of music, where he was happiest.

Unfortunately the earliest news passed on by people who had acquired accumulators and got their radio sets back in working order did not confirm Father's optimism. None of what we had heard was accurate: the French had no intention of breaking through the Siegfried Line, any more than the British planned to bomb Hamburg, let alone land on the coast of Germany. On the other hand, the first German race raids were beginning in Warsaw. Initially they were conducted clumsily, as if the perpetrators felt ashamed of this new means of tormenting people, and they had not had any practice anyway. Small private cars drove down the streets, drawing up by the pavement unexpectedly when a Jew was spotted; car doors opened, a hand reached out, crooking a finger. 'Get in!' Those who came back from such raids described the first instances of maltreatment. It was not too bad yet; the physical abuse was confined to slaps, punching, sometimes kicking. But because it was so new the victims felt it particularly keenly, regarding a slap from a German as something disgraceful. They did not yet realize that such a blow had no more moral connotation than a nudge or a kick from an animal.

At this early stage anger with the government and the army command, both of which had fled, leaving the country to its fate, was in general stronger than hatred for the Germans. Bitterly, we remembered the words of the field-marshal who had sworn that he would not let the enemy have a single button of his uniform – and nor did he, but only because the buttons remained attached to his uniform when he saved himself by escaping abroad. There was no lack of voices suggesting that we might even be better off, since the Germans would bring some order into the chaos that was Poland.

Now that the Germans had won the armed conflict against us, however, they set about losing the political war. Their execution of the first hundred innocent citizens of Warsaw in December 1939 was a crucial turning point. Within a few hours a wall of hatred had been erected between Germans and Poles, and neither side could climb it thereafter, although the Germans did show some willingness to do so in the later years of the occupation.

The first German decrees carrying the death penalty for failure to comply were posted up. The most important concerned trading in bread: anyone caught buying or selling bread at higher than pre-war prices would be shot. This prohibition made a devastating impression on us. We ate no bread for days on end, feeding on potatoes and other starchy dishes instead. However, then Henryk discovered that bread was still around and was on sale, and the buyer did not necessarily drop dead on the spot. So we began buying bread again. The decree was never rescinded, and since everyone ate and bought bread daily throughout the five years of occupation, millions of death sentences must have been incurred in the General Government area of German-ruled Polish territory for this offence alone. However, it was a long time before we were convinced that the German decrees carried no weight, and that the real danger was what could happen to you totally unexpectedly, out of a blue sky – unannounced by any rules and regulations, however fictitious.

Soon decrees applying exclusively to Jews were being published. A Jewish family could keep no more than two thousand złoty at home. Other savings and items of value must be deposited in the bank, in a blocked account. At the same time Jewish real estate had to be handed over to Germans. Naturally hardly anyone was naïve enough to give his property to the enemy of his own free will. Like everyone else, we decided to hide our valuables, although they consisted only of my father's gold watch and chain and the sum of five thousand złoty.

We argued vehemently over the best way to hide them. My father suggested certain tried and tested methods from the last war, such as boring a hole in the leg of the dining-room table and hiding the valuables there.

'And suppose they take the table away?' asked Henryk sarcastically.

'Idiot,' said Father, annoyed. 'What would they want with a table? A table like this?'

He glanced scornfully at the table. Its highly polished walnut surface had been marked by spilt liquids, and the veneer was coming away slightly in one place. In order to remove the last vestige of value from this piece of furniture, Father went over to it and pushed his finger under the loose veneer, which snapped off, leaving a strip of bare wood behind it.

'What on earth are you doing?' Mother scolded.

Henryk had another suggestion. He thought we ought to employ psychological methods and leave the watch and the money out in full view. The Germans would search high and low and never notice the valuables lying on the table.

We came to an amicable agreement: the watch was hidden under the cupboard, the chain beneath the fingerboard of Father's violin and the money was jammed into the window frame.

Although people were alarmed by the severity of the German laws, they did not lose heart, comforting themselves with the thought that the Germans could hand Warsaw over to Soviet Russia at any moment, and areas occupied just for the sake of appearances would be restored to Poland as soon as possible. No frontier had been established yet on the bend in the Vistula, and people came into the city from both sides of the river swearing that they had seen Red army troops with their own eyes in Jabłonna or Garwolin. But they were immediately followed by others who swore that they had seen, also with their own eyes, the Russians withdrawing from Vilna and Lvóv and surrendering those cities to the Germans. It was hard to decide which of these eyewitnesses should be believed.

Many Jews did not wait for the Russians to march in, but

sold their possessions in Warsaw and moved east, the only way they could still go to get away from the Germans. Almost all my musician colleagues went, and urged me to go with them. However, my family still decided to stay put.

One of those colleagues came back two days later, bruised and angry, without his rucksack and his money. He had seen five half-naked Jews strung up by their hands to the trees near the border and whipped. And he had witnessed the death of Dr Haskielewicz, who told the Germans he wanted to cross the bend. At pistol point, they had ordered him walk into the river, further and deeper into the water until he lost his footing and drowned. My colleague had merely lost his belongings and his money, and was then beaten and sent back. But most Jews, although they were robbed and ill-treated, did make it to Russia.

We were sorry for the poor man, of course, but at the same time we felt a sense of triumph: he would have done better to follow our advice and stay. Our decision was not swayed by any kind of logical consideration. The simple fact is that we decided to stay because of our fondness for Warsaw, although we could not have given any logical explanation for that either.

When I say *our* decision, I am thinking of all my loved ones except my father. If he did not leave Warsaw it was more because he didn't want to be too far from Sosnowiec, where he came from. He had never liked Warsaw, and the worse it was for us there the more he longed for and idealized Sosnowiec. Sosnowiec was the only place where life was good, where people were musical and could appreciate a good violinist. Sosnowiec was even the only place to get a glass of decent beer, because you couldn't buy anything but disgusting, undrinkable dishwater in Warsaw. After supper my father would fold his hands over his stomach, lean back, close his eyes dreamily and bore us with his monotonous recital of visions of a Sosnowiec that existed only in his fond imagination.

In those weeks of late autumn, not quite two months after the Germans took Warsaw, the city suddenly and completely unexpectedly returned to its old way of life. This upturn in its material circumstances, brought about so easily, was one more surprise to us in this most surprising of all wars, where nothing went the way we expected. The huge city, capital of a country with a population of many millions, was partly destroyed, an army of civil servants were out of work, and waves of evacuees kept coming in from Silesia, the Poznań area and Pomerania. Unexpectedly, all these people – people without a roof over their heads, without work, with the gloomiest of prospects – realized that large sums of money could be made with great ease by circumventing German decrees. The more decrees were issued, the higher the chances of earning.

Two lives began to go on side by side: an official, fictional life based on rules which forced people to work from dawn to dusk, almost without eating, and a second, unofficial life, full of fairy-tale opportunities to make a profit, with a flourishing trade in dollars, diamonds, flour, leather or even forged papers – a life lived under constant threat of the death penalty, but spent cheerfully in luxurious restaurants to which people drove in 'rickshaws'.

Not everyone was living it up, of course. Every day, when I went home in the evening, I would see a woman sitting in the same niche in the wall in Sienna Street, playing a concertina and singing sad Russian songs. She never began begging before twilight came on, probably for fear of being recognized. She wore a grey costume, probably her last, and its elegance showed that its wearer had seen better days. Her beautiful face was lifeless in the dusk, and her eyes kept staring at the same spot, somewhere high above the heads of passers-by. She had a deep, attractive singing voice, and accompanied herself well on the concertina. Her whole bearing, the way she leaned back against the wall, showed that she was a society lady forced only by the war to make her living like this. But even she earned quite well. There were always a great many coins in the ribbon-bedecked tambourine that she no doubt thought the symbol of the beggar's trade. She had placed it at her feet so that no one could be in any doubt that she was begging, and it contained some fifty-złoty notes as well as the coins.

I myself never went out until dusk, if I could help it, but for entirely different reasons. Among the many irksome regulations imposed on the Jews was one which, although unwritten, had to be observed very carefully: men of Jewish descent must bow to every German soldier. This idiotic and humiliating requirement made Henryk and me incandescent with rage. We did all we could to get around it. We took long detours in the streets, just to avoid meeting a German, and if it could not be avoided we looked away and pretended not to have seen him, although we could have got a beating for that.

My father's attitude was quite different. He sought out the longest streets for his walks, and bowed to the Germans with indescribably ironic grace, happy when one of the soldiers, misled by his beaming face, gave him a civil greeting in return and smiled as if he were a good friend. On coming home every evening he could not refrain from commenting casually on his extensive circle of acquaintances: he had only to set foot in the street, he told us, and he would be surrounded by dozens of them. He really could not resist their friendliness, and his hand was getting quite stiff from raising his hat so politely. With these words he would smile impishly, rubbing his hands with glee.

But the malice of the Germans was not to be taken lightly. It was part of a system intended to keep us in a constant state of nervous uncertainty about our future. Every few days new decrees were issued. They were apparently of no importance, but they let us know that the Germans had not forgotten us, and had no intention of doing so.

Then Jews were forbidden to travel by train. Later, we were charged four times as much as an 'Aryan' for a tram ticket. The first rumours of the construction of a ghetto began to circulate. They were rife for two days, struck despair into our hearts, and then died down again.

5 ~ Are You Jews?

Towards the end of November, when the fine days of that unusually long autumn were becoming rarer and cold showers were sweeping over the city more and more frequently, Father, Henryk and I had our first contact with the German way of death.

One evening the three of us had been out visiting a friend. We had been talking, and when I glanced at my watch I realized to my alarm that it was nearly curfew time. We needed to leave at once, although there was no chance of our getting home in time. But it was not such a great crime to be quarter of an hour late, and we could hope to get away with it.

We picked up our coats, said a hasty goodbye, and left. The streets were dark and already completely empty. The rain whipped into our faces, gusts of wind shook the signboards, the air was full of the rattling sound of metal. Turning up our coat collars, we tried to walk as fast and as quietly as possible, keeping close to the walls of the buildings. We were already halfway down Zielna Street, and it began to look as though we would reach our destination safely, when a police patrol suddenly came round a corner. We had no time to retreat or hide. We just stood there in the dazzling light of their torches, each of us trying to think of some excuse, when one of the policemen marched straight up to us and shone his torch in our faces.

'Are you Jews?' The question was purely rhetorical, since
he did not wait for us to answer. 'Right, then . . .' There was
a note of triumph in this statement of our racial origin. It
conveyed satisfaction at having tracked down such game.
Before we knew it we had been seized and turned to face
the wall of the building, while the policemen stepped back
into the road and began releasing the safety catches of their
carbines. So this was how we were to die. It would happen
in the next few seconds, and then we would lie on the pavement in our blood, with our skulls shattered, until next day.
Only then would Mother and my sisters learn what had happened and come in despair to find us. The friends we had
been visiting would reproach themselves for delaying us too
long. All these thoughts went through my head on a strange
level, as if another person were thinking them. I heard someone say out loud, 'This is the end.' Only a moment later did
I realize that I myself had spoken. At the same time I heard
loud weeping and convulsive sobbing. I turned my head, and
in the harsh torchlight I saw my father kneeling on the wet
tarmac, sobbing and begging the policemen for our lives.
How could he demean himself so? Henryk was bending over
my father, whispering to him, trying to raise him to his feet.
Henryk, my restrained brother Henryk with his eternal sarcastic smile, had something extraordinarily soft and tender
about him at that moment. I had never seen him in such a
mood before. So there must be another Henryk, one I would
understand if I only knew him, instead of being constantly
at odds with him.

I turned to the wall again. The situation had not changed.
Father was weeping, Henryk was trying to calm him, the
police were still aiming their guns at us. We could not see
them behind the wall of white light. Then suddenly, in the

fraction of a second, I instinctively sensed that death no longer threatened us. A few moments passed, and a loud voice came through the wall of light.

'What do you do for a living?'

Henryk answered for all three of us. He was amazingly self-controlled, his voice as calm as if nothing had happened. 'We're musicians.'

One of the policemen stationed himself in front of me, grabbed my coat collar and shook me in a final fit of temper, not that there was any reason for it now he had decided to let us live.

'Lucky for you I'm a musician too!'

He gave me a shove, and I stumbled back against the wall. 'Get out!'

We ran off into the dark, anxious to get out of range of their torches as fast as possible, before they could change their minds. We could hear their voices falling away behind us, engaged in violent argument. The other two were remonstrating with the one who had let us go. They thought we deserved no sympathy, since we had started the war in which Germans were dying.

For the moment they were not dying but enriching themselves. More and more frequently German gangs invaded Jewish homes, plundered them and took the furniture away in vans. Distraught householders sold their finer possessions and replaced them with worthless stuff that would tempt no one. We sold our own furniture, although out of necessity rather than fear: we were getting poorer and poorer. No one in the family was good at haggling. Regina tried but failed. As a lawyer, she had a strong sense of honesty and responsibility, and she simply could not ask, or accept, twice the price of what something was worth. She soon switched to tutorial work. Father, Mother and Halina were giving music lessons, and Henryk taught English. I was the only one who could find no way of earning my bread at that time. Sunk in apathy, all I could do was work occasionally on the orchestration of my concertino.

In the second half of November, without giving any reasons, the Germans began barricading the side streets north of Marszałkowska Street with barbed wire, and at the end of the month there was an announcement that no one could believe at first. Not in our most secret thoughts would we ever have suspected that such a thing could happen: Jews had from the first to the fifth of December to provide themselves with white armbands on which a blue Star of David must be sewn. So we were to be publicly branded as outcasts. Several centuries of humanitarian progress were to be cancelled out, and we were back in the Middle Ages.

For weeks on end the Jewish intelligentsia stayed under voluntary house arrest. No one would venture out in the street with the brand on his sleeve, and if there was simply no way to avoid leaving home we tried to pass unnoticed, walking with our eyes lowered to the ground, feeling shame and distress.

Months of bad winter weather set in, unheralded, and the cold seemed to unite with the Germans to kill people. The frosts lasted for weeks; the temperature sank lower than anyone in Poland could remember. Coal could hardly be obtained at all, and commanded fantastic prices. I remember a whole series of days when we had to stay in bed because the temperature in the flat was too cold to endure.

During the worst of that winter, numbers of Jewish deportees evacuated from the west arrived in Warsaw. That is, only some of them actually arrived: they had been loaded into cattle trucks in their places of origin, the trucks were sealed, and the people inside were sent on their way without food, water, or any means of keeping warm. It often took several days for these ghastly transports to reach Warsaw, and only then were the people let out. On some of the transports scarcely half the passengers remained alive, and they were badly frostbitten. The other half were corpses, standing frozen stiff among the rest and falling to the ground only when the living moved.

It seemed as if things could get no worse. But that was only the Jewish view; the Germans thought otherwise. True to their system of exerting pressure by gradual stages, they issued new repressive decrees in January and February of 1940. The first announced that Jews were to do two years' labour in concentration camps where we would receive 'appropriate social education', to cure us of being 'parasites on the healthy organism of the Aryan peoples'. Men aged twelve to sixty and women aged fourteen to forty-five would have to go. The second decree set out the method for registering us and taking us away. To spare themselves the trouble, the Germans were handing the job over to the Jewish Council that dealt with the community administration. We were to assist at our own execution, preparing for our downfall with our own hands, committing a kind of legally regulated suicide. The transports were to leave in the spring.

The Council decided to act to spare most of the intelligentsia. Asking a thousand złoty a head, it sent a member of the Jewish working classes as surrogate for the person supposedly registered. Of course not all the money ended up in the hands of the poor surrogates themselves: the Council officials had to live, and they lived well, with vodka and a few little delicacies.

But the transports did not leave in spring. Once again it transpired that the official German decrees were not to be taken seriously, and in fact there was a relaxation of tension in German–Jewish relations for a few months, which seemed more and more genuine as both parties were increasingly concerned with events at the front.

Spring had finally come, and now there could be no doubt that the Allies, who had spent the winter making suitable preparations, would attack Germany simultaneously from France, Belgium and Holland, break through the Siegfried Line, take the Saarland, Bavaria and northern Germany, conquer Berlin, and liberate Warsaw that summer at the latest. The whole city was in a state of happy excitement. We waited for the offensive to start as if it we were looking forward to a party. Meanwhile the Germans invaded Denmark, but in the opinion of our local politicians that meant nothing. Their armies would simply be cut off there.

On 10 May the offensive finally began, but it was a German offensive. Holland and Belgium fell. The Germans marched into France. All the more reason not to lose heart. The year 1914 was repeating itself. Why, the same people were even in command on the French side: Pétain, Weygand – excellent men of the Foch school. They could be trusted to defend themselves against the Germans as well as they did last time.

Finally, on 20 May, a colleague of mine, a violinist, came to see me after lunch. We were going to play together, reminding ourselves of a Beethoven sonata that we had not played for some time and that gave us both great pleasure. A few other friends were there, and Mother, wanting to give me a treat, had provided coffee. It was a fine, sunny day, we enjoyed the coffee and the delicious cakes Mother had baked; we were in a cheerful mood. We all knew the Germans were just outside Paris, but no one felt too much concern. After all, there was the Marne – that classic line of defence where everything must come to a standstill, the way it does in the fermata of the second section of Chopin's B minor scherzo, in a stormy tempo of quavers going on and on, more and more tempestuously, until the closing chord – at which point the Germans would retreat to their own border as vigorously as they had advanced, leading to the end of the war and an Allied victory.

After coffee, we were about to get on with our performance. I sat down at the piano, a crowd of sensitive listeners around me, people who could appreciate the pleasure I intended to give both to them and to myself. The violinist stood on my right, and to my left sat a charming young friend of Regina's who was going to turn the pages for me. What more could I ask to complete my happiness just then? We were only waiting for Halina before we began; she had gone down to the shop to make a phone call. When she came back she was carrying a newspaper: a special edition. Two words were printed on the front page in huge letters, obviously the largest the printers had available: PARIS FALLS!

I laid my head on the piano and – for the first time in this war – I burst into tears.

Intoxicated with victory and stopping for a moment to draw breath, the Germans now had time to think of us again, although it cannot be said that they had forgotten us entirely during the fighting in the west. Robberies from Jews, their compulsory evacuation, deportations for labour in Germany were going on all the time, but we had become accustomed to it. Now there was worse to be expected. In September the first transports set off for the labour camps of Bełżec and Hrubieszów. The Jews who were receiving 'appropriate social education' there stood up to their waists in water for days on end, laying improved drainage systems, and were given a hundred grams of bread and a plate of thin soup a day to keep them going. The work was not in fact, as announced, for two years but for only three months. However, that was enough to exhaust people physically and leave many of them with TB.

The men still left in Warsaw had to report for labour there: everyone was to do six days' physical labour a month. I did my utmost to avoid this work. I was worried about my fingers. I only had to suffer muscular atony, an inflammation of the joints or simply a nasty knock, and my career as a pianist would be over. Henryk saw things differently. In his view an intellectually creative person must do physical labour in order to assess his own capabilities properly, and so he did his quota of work, although it interrupted his studies.

Soon two further events affected the public mood. First, the German air offensive against England began. Second, notices went up at the entrances of streets that were later to mark the boundary of the Jewish ghetto, informing passers-by that these streets were infected by typhus and must be avoided. A little later the only Warsaw newspaper published in Polish by the Germans provided an official comment on this subject: not only were the Jews social parasites, they also spread infection. They were not, said the report, to be shut up in a ghetto; even the word ghetto was not to be used. The Germans were too cultured and magnanimous a race, said the newspaper, to confine even parasites like the Jews to ghettos, a medieval remnant unworthy of the new order in Europe. Instead, there was to be a separate Jewish quarter of the city where only Jews lived, where they would enjoy total freedom, and where they could continue to practise their racial customs and culture. Purely for hygienic reasons, this quarter was to be surrounded by a wall so that typhus and other Jewish diseases could not spread to other parts of the city. This humanitarian report was illustrated by a small map showing the precise borders of the ghetto.

At least we could console ourselves that our street was already in the ghetto area, and we did not have to look for another flat. Jews who lived outside the area were in an unfortunate situation. They had to pay exorbitant sums in key money and look for a new roof over their heads in the last weeks of October. The luckiest found rooms available in Sienna Street, which was to be the Champs-Elysées of the ghetto, or moved into the nearby area. Others were condemned to squalid holes in the infamous areas of Gęsia, Smocza and Zamenhof Streets, which had been occupied by the Jewish proletariat from time immemorial.

The gates of the ghetto were closed on 15 November. I had business that evening at the far end of Sienna Street, not far from Żelazna Street. It was drizzling, but still unusually warm for the time of year. The dark streets were swarming with figures wearing white armbands. They were all in an agitated state, running back and forth like animals put into a cage and not yet used to it. Women were wailing and children were crying in terror as they perched beside the walls of the buildings, on mounds of bedding gradually getting wet and dirty from the filth in the streets. These were Jewish families who had been forcibly put behind the ghetto walls at the last minute, and had no hope of finding shelter. Half a million people had to find somewhere to lay their heads in an already over-populated part of the city, which scarcely had room for more than a hundred thousand.

Looking down the dark street, I saw floodlights illuminating the new wooden grating: the ghetto gate, beyond which free people lived – unconfined, with adequate space, in the same city of Warsaw. But no Jew could pass through that gate any longer.

At one point, someone took my hand. It was a friend of my father's, another musician, and like my father a man of a cheerful, friendly nature.

'Well, how about this, then?' he asked with a nervous laugh, his hand describing an arc that took in the crowds of people, the dirty walls of the houses, wet with rain, and the ghetto walls and gate visible in the distance.

'How about it?' I said. 'They want to finish us off.'

But the old gentleman didn't share my opinion, or did not want to. He gave another, slightly forced laugh, patted me on the back and cried, 'Oh, don't you worry!' Then he took hold of the button on my coat, put his red-cheeked face close to mine, and said, with either genuine or pretended conviction, 'They'll soon let us out. We only need America to know.'

6 ~ Dancing in Chłodna Street

Today, as I look back on other, more terrible memories, my experiences of the Warsaw ghetto from November 1940 to July 1942, a period of almost two years, merge into a single image as if they had lasted only a single day. Hard as I try, I cannot break it up into smaller sections that would impose some chronological order on it, as you usually do when writing a journal.

Naturally some things happened at the time, as well as before and after it, that were common knowledge and easy to grasp. The Germans went hunting human game for use as workhorses, just as they did all over Europe. Perhaps the only difference was that in the Warsaw ghetto these hunts suddenly stopped in the spring of 1942. In a few months' time the Jewish prey was to serve other purposes, and like other game needed a close season, so that the big show hunts would be all the better and cause no disappointment. We Jews were robbed, just as the French, Belgians, Norwegians and Greeks were robbed, but with the difference that we were robbed more systematically and in a strictly official way. Germans who were not part of the system had no access to the ghetto and no right to steal for themselves. The German police were authorized to steal by a decree issued by the governor-general in line with the law on theft, published by the government of the Reich.

In 1941 Germany invaded Russia. In the ghetto we held

our breath as we followed the course of this new offensive. At first we believed erroneously that the Germans would finally lose now; later we felt despair and ever-increasing doubt about the fate of mankind and ourselves as Hitler's troops advanced further into Russia. Then again, when the Germans ordered all Jewish fur coats to be handed in on pain of the death penalty, we were pleased to think they could not be doing particularly well if their victory depended on silver fox and beaver furs.

The ghetto was closing in. Street by street, the Germans were reducing its area. In exactly the same way, Germany shifted the borders of the European countries it had subdued, appropriating province after province; it was as if the Warsaw ghetto were no less important than France, and the exclusion of Złota Street and Zielna Street as significant for the expansion of German *Lebensraum* as the separation of Alsace and Lorraine from French territory.

However, these outside incidents were entirely unimportant compared to the one significant fact that constantly occupied our minds, every hour and every minute of the time we spent in the ghetto: we were shut in.

I think it would have been psychologically easier to bear if we had been more obviously imprisoned – locked in a cell, for instance. That kind of imprisonment clearly, indubitably, defines a human being's relationship to reality. There is no mistaking your situation: the cell is a world in itself, containing only your own imprisonment, never interlocking with the distant world of freedom. You can dream of that world if you have the time and inclination; however, if you don't think of it, it will not force itself on your notice of its own accord. It is not always there before your eyes, tormenting you with reminders of the free life you have lost.

The reality of the ghetto was all the worse just because it had the appearance of freedom. You could walk out into the street and maintain the illusion of being in a perfectly normal city. The armbands branding us as Jews did not bother us, because we were all wearing them, and after some time living in the ghetto I realized that I had become thoroughly used to them – so much so that when I dreamed of my Aryan friends I saw them wearing armbands, as if that white strip of fabric was as essential a part of the human wardrobe as a tie. However, the streets of the ghetto – and those streets alone – ended in walls. I very often went out walking at random, following my nose, and unexpectedly came up against one of these walls. They barred my way when I wanted to walk on and there was no logical reason to stop me. Then the part of the street on the other side of the wall would suddenly seem to be the place I loved and needed most in all the world, a place where things must be going on at this very moment that I would give anything to see – but it was no use. I would turn back, crushed, and I went on like this day after day, always with the same sense of despair.

Even in the ghetto you could go to a restaurant or a café. You met friends there, and nothing seemed to prevent you from creating as pleasant an atmosphere as in a restaurant or café anywhere else. However, the moment inevitably came when one of your friends would let slip a remark to the effect that it would be nice for this little party, engaged in such pleasant conversation, to go on an excursion somewhere one fine Sunday, say Otwock. It's summer, he might say, and nice weather, the warm spell seems to be holding – and there'd be nothing to stop you carrying out such a simple plan, even if you felt like doing it there and then. You would only have to pay the bill for coffee and cakes, go out into the street, walk to the station with your laughing, cheerful companions, buy tickets and get on the suburban train. All the conditions to create a perfect illusion existed – until you came up against the boundary of the walls . . .

The period of nearly two years I spent in the ghetto reminds me, when I think of it, of a childhood experience which lasted a much shorter time. I was to have my appendix removed. The operation was expected to be routine, nothing to worry about. It would be performed in a week's time; the date was agreed with the doctors and a hospital room had been reserved. Hoping to ease the wait for me, my parents went to great trouble to fill the week before my operation with treats. We went out to eat ice-cream every day and then to the cinema or theatre; I was given lots of books and toys, everything my heart could desire. It looked as if there was nothing more I needed to complete my happiness. But I still remember that all week, whether I was at the pictures, in the theatre or eating ices, even during amusements that called for great concentration, I was not free for a single moment of the itch of fear in the pit of my stomach, an unconscious, persistent fear of what would happen when the day of the operation finally came.

The same instinctive fear never left the people in the ghetto for almost two years. Compared to the time that followed, these were years of relative calm, but they changed our lives into an endless nightmare, since we felt with our entire being that something dreadful would happen at any moment – we were just not sure yet what danger threatened, and where it would come from.

In the morning I usually went out straight after breakfast. My daily ritual included a long walk along Miła Street to a dark, obscure den where the family of the caretaker Jehuda Zyskind lived. Under ghetto conditions, leaving the house, a perfectly normal activity, took on the character of a ceremony, particularly during the street hunts. First you had to visit neighbours, listen to their troubles and complaints, and thus find out what was going on in the city today: were there raids, had they heard of any blockades, was Chłodna Street guarded? When you had done that you left the building, but you had to repeat your questions in the street, stopping passers-by coming towards you and then asking again at every street corner. Only such precautions could ensure, with relative certainty, that you would not be picked up.

The ghetto was divided into a large ghetto and a small ghetto. After further reduction in size the small ghetto, consisting of Wielka, Sienna, Żelazna and Chłodna Streets, had only one link with the large ghetto, from the corner of Żelazna Street and over Chłodna Street. The large ghetto comprised the whole northern part of Warsaw, containing a great many narrow, evil-smelling streets and alleys and crammed with Jews living in poverty in dirty, cramped conditions. The small ghetto was crowded too, but not unreasonably so. Three or four people lived to a room, and you could walk down the streets without bumping into other pedestrians if you tacked and manoeuvred skilfully. Even if you did come into physical contact it was not too dangerous, since the people living in the small ghetto were mainly from the intelligentsia and the prosperous middle class; they were relatively free of vermin, and did their best to exterminate the vermin everyone picked up in the large ghetto. It was only when you had left Chłodna Street that the nightmare began – and you needed luck and a feeling for the right moment to get to that point in the first place.

Chłodna Street was in the 'Aryan' quarter of the city, and there was much coming and going of cars, trams and pedestrians. Allowing the Jewish population along Żelazna Street from the small to the large ghetto, and the other way around, meant the traffic had to be stopped as people crossed Chłodna Street. This was inconvenient for the Germans, so Jews were allowed to go through as seldom as possible.

If you walked down Żelazna Street, you could see a crowd of people on the corner of Chłodna Street at quite a distance. Those with urgent business were treading nervously from foot to foot on the spot, waiting for the policemen to be kind enough to stop the traffic. It was up to them to decide whether Chłodna Street was empty enough and Żelazna Street crammed enough to let the Jews over. When that moment came the guards moved apart, and an impatient, close-packed crowd of people surged towards each other from both sides, colliding, flinging one another to the ground, treading other people underfoot to get away from the dangerous vicinity of the Germans as quickly as possible and back inside the two ghettos. Then the chain of guards closed again, and the waiting began once more.

As the crowd grew so did its agitation, nervousness and restlessness, for the German guards were bored at their posts here, and tried to amuse themselves as best they could. One of their favourite entertainments was dancing. Musicians were fetched from the nearby side streets – the number of street bands grew with the general misery. The soldiers chose people out of the waiting crowd whose appearance they thought particularly comic and ordered them to dance waltzes. The musicians took up a position by the wall of a building, space was cleared in the road, and one of the policemen acted as conductor by hitting the musicians if they played too slowly. Others supervised the conscientious performance of the dances. Couples of cripples, old people, the very fat or the very thin had to whirl about in circles before the eyes of the horrified crowd. Short people or children were made to partner the strikingly tall. The Germans stood around this 'dance floor', roaring with laughter and shouting, 'Faster! Go on, faster! Everybody dance!'

If the choice of couples was particularly successful and amusing the dancing went on longer. The crossing opened, closed and opened again, but the unfortunate dancers had to go on skipping about in waltz-time – panting, weeping with exhaustion, struggling to keep going, in the vain hope of mercy.

Only once I was safely across Chłodna Street did I see the ghetto as it really was. Its people had no capital, no secret valuables; they earned their bread by trading. The further you went into the labyrinth of narrow alleys, the livelier and more urgent the trade was. Women with children clinging to their skirts would accost passers-by, offering a few cakes for sale on a piece of cardboard. They represented the entire fortune of such women, and whether their children had a small piece of black bread to eat that evening depended on their sale. Old Jews, emaciated beyond recognition, tried to draw your attention to some sort of rags from which they hoped to make money. Young men traded in gold and notes, fighting bitter and rancorous battles over battered watch-cases, the ends of chains, or worn and dirty dollar bills that they held up to the light, announcing that they were flawed and worth almost nothing, although the sellers insisted passionately that they were 'almost like new'.

The horse-drawn trams known as *konhellerki* made their

way through the crowded streets with a clattering and ringing of bells, the horses and shafts dividing the crowd of human bodies as a boat makes its way through the water. The nickname came from the tram proprietors Kon and Heller, two Jewish magnates who were in the service of the Gestapo and did a flourishing trade through it. The fares were quite high, so only the prosperous took these trams, coming into the centre of the ghetto solely on business. When they got out at the tram stops they tried to be as quick as possible in making their way through the streets to the shop or office where they had an appointment, taking another tram immediately afterwards so as to leave this terrible quarter at speed.

Merely getting from the tram stop to the nearest shop was not easy. Dozens of beggars lay in wait for this brief moment of encounter with a prosperous citizen, mobbing him by pulling at his clothes, barring his way, begging, weeping, shouting, threatening. But it was foolish for anyone to feel sympathy and give a beggar something, for then the shouting would rise to a howl. That signal would bring more and more wretched figures streaming up from all sides, and the good Samaritan would find himself besieged, hemmed in by ragged apparitions spraying him with tubercular saliva, by children covered with oozing sores who were pushed into his path, by gesticulating stumps of arms, blinded eyes, toothless, stinking open mouths, all begging for mercy at this, the last moment of their lives, as if their end could be delayed only by instant support.

To get to the centre of the ghetto you had to go down Karmelicka Street, the only way there. It was downright impossible not to brush against other people in the street here. The dense crowd of humanity was not walking but pushing and shoving its way forward, forming whirlpools in front of stalls and bays outside doorways. A chilly odour of decay was given off by unaired bedclothes, old grease and rubbish rotting in the streets. At the slightest provocation the crowd would become panic-stricken, rushing from one side of the street to the other, choking, pressing close, shouting and cursing. Karmelicka Street was a particularly dangerous place: prison cars drove down it several times a day. They were taking prisoners, invisible behind grey steel sides and small opaque glass windows, from the Pawiak gaol to the Gestapo centre in Szuch Alley, and on the return journey they brought back what remained of them after their interrogation: bloody scraps of humanity with broken bones and beaten kidneys, their fingernails torn out. The escort of these cars allowed no one near them, although the cars themselves were armoured. When they turned into Karmelicka Street, which was so crowded that with the best will in the world people could not take refuge in doorways, the Gestapo men would lean out and beat the crowd indiscriminately with truncheons. This would not have been especially dangerous had they been ordinary rubber truncheons, but those used by the Gestapo men were studded with nails and razor blades.

Jehuda Zyskind lived on Miła Street, not far from Carmelita Street. He looked after his building and when necessary acted as carrier, driver, trader and smuggler of goods over the ghetto wall. With his shrewd mind and the physical strength of his huge frame, he earned money wherever he could to feed his family. It was such a large family that I could not even guess its full extent. Apart from these everyday occupations, however, Zyskind was an idealistic socialist. He kept in touch with the socialist organization, smuggled secret press reports into the ghetto and tried to form cells there, although he found this last hard going. He treated me with kindly contempt, which he thought the proper approach to artists, people who were no use as conspirators. All the same, he liked me, and allowed me to call every morning and read the secret announcements that had come by radio, fresh off the press. When I think of him today, over the years of horror which divide me from the time when he was still alive and could spread his message, I admire his unyielding will. Jehuda was a determined optimist. However bad the radio news, he could always put a good interpretation on it. Once, when I had been reading the latest news, I brought my hand down in desperation on the rag of newsprint and sighed, 'Well, you have to admit it's all over now.' Jehuda smiled, reached for a cigarette, made himself comfortable in his chair and replied, 'Oh, but you don't understand, Mr Szpilman!' Whereupon he launched into one of his political lectures. Much of what he said I understood even less, but he had a way of talking and such an infectious belief that everything really was for the best in this best of all possible worlds that I would find I had gone over to his way of thinking, I had no idea how and when. I always came away from him feeling fortified and comforted. Not until I was home, lying in bed and going over the political news once more, did I conclude that his arguments were nonsense. But next morning I would visit him once again, and he would manage to persuade me I was wrong, and I left with an injection of optimism that lasted until evening and kept me going. Jehuda lasted until the winter of 1942, when he was caught *in flagrante*, with piles of secret material on the table while he, his wife and children sorted them. They were all shot there and then, even little Symche, aged three.

It was difficult for me to retain any hope once Zyskind

had been murdered, and I had no one to explain everything properly to me! Only now do I know that I was wrong, and so were news reports of the day, while Zyskind was right. Unlikely as it seemed at the time, everything turned out as he had predicted.

I always went the same way home: Karmelicka Street, Leszno Street, Żelazna Street. On the way I would look in briefly to see friends and deliver, by word of mouth, the news I had gleaned from Zyskind. Then I went down Nowolipki Street to help Henryk carry his basket of books home.

Henryk's life was a hard one. He had chosen it himself and had no intention of changing it, believing that it would be contemptible to live in any other way. Friends who valued his cultural qualities advised him to join the Jewish police, as most young men from the intelligentsia did; you could be safe there, and if you were resourceful you could earn quite well. Henryk would have nothing to do with this idea. He became quite angry, and took it as an insult. Adopting his usual strictly upright attitude, he said he was not going to work with bandits. Our friends' feelings were hurt, but Henryk began going to Nowolipki Street every morning with a basket full of books. He traded with them, standing there dripping with sweat in summer and shivering in the winter frosts, inflexible, obstinately true to his own ideas: if, as an intellectual, he could have no other contact with books then at least he would have this, and he would not sink any lower.

When Henryk and I got home with his basket the others were usually there, just waiting for us to begin the midday meal. Mother was particularly insistent on our eating together: this was her domain, and in her own way she was trying to give us something to cling to. She made sure the table was prettily laid and the tablecloth and napkins clean.

She powdered her face lightly before we sat down, tidied her hair and glanced in the mirror to see if she looked elegant. She smoothed her dress down with nervous gestures, but she could not smooth away the little wrinkles round her eyes – they were more and more obvious as the months went by – or keep the sprinkling of grey in her hair from beginning to turn white.

When we were seated at the table she brought soup in from the kitchen, and as she ladled it out she would set the conversation going. She tried to make sure no one mentioned unpleasant subjects, but if one of us did commit such a social *faux pas* she interrupted gently.

'It will all pass over, you wait and see,' she would say, changing the subject at once.

Father was not inclined to brood, and was more likely to try overwhelming us with good news instead. Supposing there had been a race raid and a dozen men had been freed later in return for bribes, he would claim, beaming, to have it on the best of authority that all men either over or under forty, either with or without an education, had been freed for one reason or another – however it might be, this was always supposed to be very encouraging. If there was no denying that the news from the city was bad, he sat down to table looking depressed, but the soup soon restored his spirits. During the second course, which usually consisted of vegetables, he cheered up and launched into carefree conversation.

Henryk and Regina were usually both deep in thought. Regina would be preparing mentally for the work she did in a lawyer's office in the afternoons. She earned tiny sums, but worked with as much probity as if she were being paid thousands. If Henryk shook off his gloomy thoughts it was only to start an argument with me. He would stare at me for a while in astonishment, then shrug his shoulders and growl, finally venting his feelings, 'Really, only a born fool would wear ties like Władek's!'

'Fool yourself! Idiot too!' I would reply, and our quarrel was in full swing. He did not appreciate the fact that I had to be well dressed when I played the piano in public. He didn't really want to understand me and my affairs. Now that he has been dead so long I know we loved each other in our own way, in spite of everything, although we were always getting on each other's nerves, probably because we were very similar characters at heart.

I understood Halina least. She was the only one who did not seem like a member of our family. She was reserved and never showed her thoughts and feelings, or told us what she did when she left the house. She would come home as impassive and indifferent as ever. Day after day she simply sat at the dining table without showing the slightest interest in what might happen. I can't say what she was really like, and now I can never find out any more about her.

Our midday meal was very simple. We almost never had meat, and Mother made the other dishes very economically. All the same, they were lavish compared to what most people in the ghetto had on their plates.

In winter, on a damp December day when the snow had turned to slush underfoot and a keen wind blew down the streets, I happened to see an old 'grabber' eating his own midday meal. In the ghetto, 'grabber' was our name for some-one sunk in such dire poverty that he had to steal to keep alive. Such people would rush at a passer-by carrying a pack-age, snatch it and run off, hoping to find something edible inside.

I was crossing Bank Square; a few steps ahead of me a poor woman was carrying a can wrapped in newspaper, and between me and the woman a ragged old man was dragging himself along. His shoulders bowed, he was shivering with cold as he made his way through the slush, in shoes with holes in them that showed his purple feet. Suddenly the old man lunged forward, seized the can and tried to tear it away from the woman. I don't know whether he wasn't strong enough, or whether she clung to the can too firmly, but in any case, instead of ending up in his hands the can fell on the pavement, and thick, steaming soup poured out into the dirty street.

All three of us stood rooted to the spot. The woman was speechless with horror. The grabber stared at the can, then at the woman, and let out a groan that sounded like a whimper. Then, suddenly, he threw himself down full length in the slush, lapping the soup straight from the pavement, cupping his hands round it on both sides so that none of it would escape him, and ignoring the woman's reaction as she kicked at his head, howling, and tore at her hair in despair.

7 ~ A Fine Gesture by Mrs K

In the early spring of 1942 human-hunting in the ghetto, previously a systematically conducted pursuit, suddenly stopped. If it had happened two years earlier people would have been relieved, seeing it as a reason for rejoicing; they would have cherished the illusion that this was a change for the better. But now, after two and a half years living at close quarters with the Germans, no one could be deluded. If they had stopped the hunts it was only because they had thought up another and better idea for tormenting us. The question was, what sort of idea? People engaged in the most fantastic suppositions, and instead of feeling calmer they were twice as anxious as before.

At least we could sleep easy at home for the time being, and Henryk and I did not have to camp out all night in the doctors' surgery at the slightest alarm. It was very uncomfortable there. Henryk slept on the operating table, I slept in the gynaecological chair, and when I woke in the morning my eyes would see the X-ray pictures hung up above my head to dry, showing diseased hearts, tubercular lungs, gall bladders full of stones, broken bones. However, our doctor friend, who was head of this partnership, had been right in saying that even during the most ferocious nocturnal raid it would never enter the heads of the Gestapo to search the surgery, so it was the only place where we could sleep safely.

This apparently total calm lasted until one Friday in the

second half of the month of April, when a gale of fear swept unexpectedly through the ghetto. There seemed no reason for it, since as soon as you asked people why they were so frightened and distressed and what they thought was going to happen, no one had a concrete answer. None the less, directly after midday all the shops were closed and people hid at home.

I was not sure what would be happening at the café. I went to the Sztuka as usual, but it too was shut. I felt particularly nervous on my way home when, despite all the enquiries I made of usually well-informed acquaintances, I simply could not find out what was going on. Nobody knew.

We all stayed up, fully clothed, until eleven, but then we decided to go to bed, since everything was quiet outside. We were almost sure the panic had been the result of unfounded rumours. Father was the first to go out in the morning. He came back a few minutes later, pale and alarmed: the Germans had been into a great many buildings overnight, and had dragged some seventy men out into the street and shot them. So far no one had collected the corpses.

What did this mean? What had those people done to the Germans? We were horrified and indignant.

The answer did not come until that afternoon, when posters were pasted up in the empty streets. The German authorities informed us that they had been obliged to cleanse our part of the city of 'undesirable elements', but their action would not affect the loyal part of the population: shops and cafés must be opened again at once, and people were to resume their ordinary lives, which were not in any danger.

The following month certainly passed peacefully. It was May, and even in the ghetto lilac blossomed here and there in the few little gardens, while flower clusters in bud hung from the acacias, turning paler every day. Just as the flowers were about to come out fully the Germans remembered us. But this time there was a difference: they did not plan to deal with us themselves. Instead, they were handing over the duty of human-hunting to the Jewish police and the Jewish labour bureau.

Henryk had been right when he refused to join the police and described them as bandits. They had been recruited mainly from young men in the more prosperous classes of society, and a number of our acquaintances were among them. We were all the more horrified when we saw that men with whom we used to shake hands, whom we had treated as friends, men who had still been decent people not long ago, were now so despicable. You could have said, perhaps, that they had caught the Gestapo spirit. As soon as they put on their uniforms and police caps and picked up their rubber truncheons, their natures changed. Now their ultimate ambition was to be in close touch with the Gestapo, to be useful to Gestapo officers, parade down the street with them, show off their knowledge of the German language and vie with their masters in the harshness of their dealings with the Jewish population. That did not prevent them from forming a police jazz band which, incidentally, was excellent.

During the human-hunt in May they surrounded the streets with the professionalism of racially pure SS men. They strode about in their elegant uniforms, shouting in loud and brutal voices in imitation of the Germans and beating people with their rubber truncheons.

I was still at home when Mother came running in with news of the hunt: they had picked up Henryk. I decided to get him away at any price, although all I could count on was my popularity as a pianist; my own papers were not in order.

I made my way through a series of cordons, getting picked up and then being allowed to go again, until I reached the labour bureau building. There were a number of men in front of it being herded in from all directions by the police, who acted as sheepdogs. The flock kept growing as new parties were brought in from the nearby streets. With difficulty, I managed to make my way through to the deputy director of the labour bureau and get a promise that Henryk would be home again before dark.

And so he was, although – much to my own surprise – he was furious with me. He thought I ought not to have demeaned myself by petitioning such low specimens of humanity as the police and the labour bureau staff.

'So you'd rather they'd taken you away, would you?'

'That's nothing to do with you!' he growled back. 'It was me they wanted, not you. Why go interfering in other people's business?'

I shrugged my shoulders. What's the point of arguing with a madman?

That evening it was announced that curfew would be postponed until midnight, so that the families of those 'sent for labour' would have time to bring them blankets, a change of underwear and food for the journey. This 'magnanimity' on the part of the Germans was truly touching, and the Jewish police made much of it in an effort to win our confidence.

Not until much later did I learn that the thousand men rounded up in the ghetto had been taken straight to the camp at Treblinka, so that the Germans could test the efficiency of the newly built gas chambers and crematorium furnaces.

Another month of peace and quiet passed, and then, one June evening, there was a bloodbath in the ghetto. We were too far away to have any idea of what was about to happen. It was hot, and after supper we pulled up the blinds that shaded our dining room and opened the windows wide to get a breath of the cooler evening air. The Gestapo vehicle had driven past the house opposite at such speed, and the warning shots came so fast, that before we could jump up from the table and run to the window the doors of that building were already open, and we could hear the SS men shouting inside. The windows had been opened too, and were dark, but we could hear a great deal of disturbance behind them. Alarmed faces emerged from the gloom and quickly withdrew again. As the jackbooted Germans marched upstairs the lights went on, floor by floor. A businessman's family lived in the flat directly opposite ours; we knew them well by sight. When the light went on there too and SS men in helmets stormed into the room, machine pistols ready to fire, the people inside were sitting around their table just as we had been seated at ours a moment ago. They were frozen with horror. The NCO leading the detachment took this as a personal insult. Speechless with indignation, he stood there in silence, scanning the people at the table. Only after a moment or so did he shout, in a towering rage, 'Stand up!'

They rose to their feet as fast as they could, all except for the head of the family, an old man with lame legs. The NCO was seething with anger. He went up to the table, braced his arms on it, stared hard at the cripple, and growled for the second time, 'Stand up!'

The old man gripped the arms of his chair to support himself and made desperate efforts to stand, but in vain. Before we realized what was going on, the Germans had seized the sick man, picked him up, armchair and all, carried the chair on to the balcony, and thrown it out into the street from the third floor.

Mother screamed and closed her eyes. Father shrank far back from the window into the room. Halina hurried over to him, and Regina put her arm around Mother's shoulders, saying quite loudly and very clearly, in an authoritative tone, 'Quiet!'

Henryk and I could not tear ourselves away from the window. We saw the old man still hanging in his armchair in the air for a second or two, and then he fell out of it. We heard the chair fall to the road separately, and the smack of a human body landing on the stones of the pavement. We stood there in silence, rooted to the spot, unable to move back or look away from the scene in front of us.

Meanwhile the SS had already taken a couple of dozen men from the building out into the street. They switched on the headlights of their car, forced their prisoners to stand in the beam, started the engines and made the men run ahead of them in the white cone of light. We heard convulsive screaming from the windows of the building, and a volley of machine-gun fire from the car. The men running ahead of it fell one by one, lifted into the air by the bullets, turning somersaults and describing a circle, as if the passage from life to death consisted of an extremely difficult and compli-cated leap. Only one of them succeeded in dodging aside and out of the cone of light. He ran with all his might, and it looked as if he would reach the street that intersected with ours. But the car had a swivelling floodlight mounted on top for such contingencies. It flared into light, sought the fugitive, there was another volley, and now it was his turn to leap into the air. He raised his arms above his head, arched back-wards as he jumped, and fell on his back.

The SS men all got into the car and drove away over the dead bodies. The vehicle swayed slightly as it passed over them, as if it were bumping over shallow potholes.

That night about a hundred people were shot in the ghetto, but this operation did not make nearly as much of an impression as the first. The shops and cafés were open as usual next day.

There was something else to interest people at this time: among their other daily activities, the Germans had taken to making films. We wondered why. They would burst into a restaurant and tell the waiters to lay a table with the finest food and drink. Then they ordered the customers to laugh, eat and drink, and they were captured on celluloid amusing themselves in this way. The Germans filmed performances of operetta at the Femina cinema in Leszno Street, and the symphony concerts conducted by Marian Neuteich given at the same venue once a week. They insisted that the chairman of the Jewish Council should hold a luxurious reception and invite all the prominent people in the ghetto, and they filmed this reception too. One day, finally, they herded a certain number of men and women into the public baths, told them to get undressed and bathe in the same room, and they filmed this curious scene in detail. Only much, much later did I discover that these films were intended for the German population at home in the Reich and abroad. The Germans were making these films before they liquidated the ghetto, to give the lie to any disconcerting rumours if news of the action should reach the outside world. They would show how well off the Jews of Warsaw were – and how immoral and despicable they were too, hence the scenes of Jewish men and women sharing the baths, immodestly stripping naked in front of each other.

At more or less the same time, increasingly alarming rumours began to circulate in the ghetto at ever shorter intervals, although as usual they were unfounded and you could never find anyone who was the source of them, or who could provide the slightest confirmation that they were based on fact. One day, for instance, people began talking about the dreadful conditions in the Łódź ghetto, where the Jews had been forced to put their own iron currency into circulation – you could not buy anything with it, and now they were dying of starvation in their thousands. Some took this news very much to heart; with others it went in one ear and out the other. After a while people stopped talking about Łódź and began on Lublin and Tarnów, where apparently the Jews were being poisoned with gas, although no one could really believe that story. More credible was the rumour that the Jewish ghettos in Poland were to be limited to four: Warsaw, Lublin, Cracow and Radom. Then, for a change, rumours began going around suggesting that the people in the Warsaw ghetto were to be resettled in the east and were to leave in transports of six thousand people a day. In some people's opinion this action would have been carried out a long time ago but for that mysterious conference of the Jewish Council which succeeded in persuading the Gestapo (undoubtedly through bribery) not to resettle us.

On 18 July, a Saturday, Goldfeder and I were playing in a concert at the Café Pod Fontanną (Fountain) in Leszno Street, a benefit for the famous pianist Leon Boruński who had once won the Chopin competition. Now he had tuberculosis and was living in destitution in the ghetto in Otwock. The garden of the café was crammed. About four hundred people of the social élite and would-be élite had attended. Scarcely anyone could remember the last function on such a scale, but if there was excitement among the audience it was for other reasons entirely: the fine ladies of the wealthy classes and the smart social parvenus were all agog to discover whether Mrs L would speak to Mrs K today. Both these ladies engaged in charity work, playing an active part in the operations of the house committees that had been formed in many of the more prosperous buildings to help the poor. This charity work was particularly enjoyable because it involved frequent balls at which people danced, amused themselves and drank, donating the proceeds to charitable purposes.

The cause of the ill feeling between the two ladies was an incident in the Sztuka café a few days earlier. They were both very pretty in their different ways, and they heartily disliked each other, making great efforts to entice one another's admirers away. The greatest prize among these was Maurycy Kohn, a railway proprietor and Gestapo agent, a man with the attractive and sensitive face of an actor.

That evening both ladies had been enjoying themselves in the Sztuka. They sat at the bar, each in the small circle of her admirers, trying to outdo one another in ordering the most recherché drinks and getting the accordionist of the jazz band to play the best of the hit tunes at their tables. Mrs L left first. She had no idea that while she was inside a starving woman had dragged herself along the street, and then collapsed and died just outside the door to the bar. Dazzled by the light from the café, Mrs L stumbled over the dead woman as she left. On seeing the corpse she fell into convulsions and could not be calmed. Not so Mrs K, who had now been told of the incident. When she too went out of the door she uttered a shriek of horror, but then immediately, as if overcome by the depth of her sympathy, went over to the dead woman, took five hundred złoty from her own handbag and gave the money to Kohn, who was just behind her. 'Please deal with this for me,' she asked him. 'See she gets a decent burial.'

Whereupon one of the ladies of her circle whispered, loud enough for everyone to hear, 'An angel, as always!'

Mrs L could not forgive Mrs K for this. She described her the next day as 'a low-class slut', and said she was never going to speak to her again. Today both ladies were to be at the Pod Fontanną café, and the *jeunesse dorée* of the ghetto was waiting curiously to see what would happen when they met.

The first half of the concert was now over, and Goldfeder and I went out into the street to smoke a cigarette at leisure. We had made friends and had been appearing as a duo for a year; he is dead now, although his prospects of survival looked better than mine at the time. He was an excellent pianist and also a lawyer. He had graduated from the conservatory and the university faculty of law at the same time, but he was extremely self-critical and had come to the conclusion that he would never be a really top-ranking pianist, so he had entered the law instead; only during the war did he become a pianist again.

He was outstandingly popular in pre-war Warsaw, thanks to his intelligence, his personal charm and his elegance. Later, he managed to escape the ghetto and survive for two years hidden in the home of the writer Gabriel Karski. A week before the Soviet army invaded, he was shot by Germans in a little town not far from the ruins of Warsaw.

We smoked and talked, feeling less exhausted with each breath we took. It had been a beautiful day. The sun had already disappeared behind the buildings; only the roofs and windows of the upper storeys still glowed crimson. The deep blue of the sky was fading to a paler colour; swallows swooped across it. The crowds in the street were thinning out, and even they looked less dirty and unhappy than usual as they walked by, bathed in the blue, crimson and dull gold evening light.

Then we saw Kramsztyk walking towards us. We both felt pleased: we must get him into the second half of the concert. He had promised to paint my portrait, and I wanted to discuss the details with him.

However, he would not be persuaded to come in. He seemed subdued, immersed in his own gloomy thoughts. A little while ago he had heard, from a reliable source, that this time the forthcoming resettlement of the ghetto was unavoidable: the German extermination commando was already poised for action on the other side of the wall, ready to begin operations.

8 ~ An Anthill Under Threat

Around this time Goldfeder and I were trying to organize a midday concert for the anniversary of the formation of our duo. It was to be in the garden of the Sztuka on Saturday, 25 July 1942. We were optimists. Our hearts were set on this concert, and we had gone to a lot of trouble preparing for it. Now, on the eve of the event, we just could not believe it was not to take place. We simply trusted that the rumours of resettlement would turn out to be unfounded once more. On Sunday, 19 July I played again in the garden of a café in Nowolipki Street, never guessing that this was to be my last performance in the ghetto. The garden café was full, but the mood was rather sombre.

After the performance I looked in at the Sztuka. It was late, and there was no one left in the café; only the staff were still busy with the final chores of the day. I sat down for a moment with the manager. He was in a gloomy mood, giving orders without any conviction, as if for form's sake.

'Are you getting the place ready for our concert on Saturday yet?' I asked.

He looked at me as if he didn't know what I was talking about. Then his face showed ironic sympathy for my ignorance of the events that had given a completely different turn to the fate of the ghetto.

'You really think we'll still be alive on Saturday?' he enquired, leaning over the table towards me.

'I'm sure we will!' I replied.

At this, as if my answer had opened up new prospects of safety, and that safety depended on me, he grasped my hand and said fervently, 'Well, if we really are still alive, you can order anything you like for supper here on Saturday, at my expense, and –' Here he hesitated briefly, but then decided to do the thing properly, and added, 'And you can order the best the Sztuka cellars can offer – on me too, and as much of it as you want!'

According to the rumours, the resettlement 'action' was to start on Sunday night. However, the night passed quietly, and people were encouraged on Monday morning. Perhaps, yet again, there was nothing in the rumours?

Towards evening, however, panic broke out once more: according to the latest information, the action was to begin tonight with the resettlement of the occupants of the small ghetto, and this time there was no doubt about it. Agitated crowds of people carrying bundles and large trunks and accompanied by children began moving from the small to the large ghetto, crossing the bridge the Germans had built over Chłodna Street to cut us off from the last chance of contact with the Aryan quarter. They were hoping to get clear of the threatened area before curfew. In line with our family's fatalistic attitude, we stayed put. Late in the evening the neighbours heard news from Polish police headquarters that an alert had been issued. So something bad really was about to happen. I could not sleep until four in the morning, and stayed up sitting by the open window. But that night passed peacefully too.

On Tuesday morning Goldfeder and I went to the Jewish Council's administrative body. We had not yet lost hope that everything might work out somehow, and we wanted to get

the Council's official information about German plans for
the ghetto over the next few days. We had almost reached
the building when an open car drove past us. Sitting in it,
surrounded by police, pale and bare-headed, was Colonel
Kon, head of the community health department. Many other
Jewish functionaries had been arrested at the same time, and
a hunt had begun in the streets.

The afternoon of the same day something happened that
shook the whole of Warsaw, on both sides of the wall. A
well-known Polish surgeon called Dr Raszeja, a leading
expert in his field and a professor at Poznań University, had
been called to the ghetto to perform a difficult operation.
The German police headquarters in Warsaw had given him
a pass to let him into the ghetto, but once he had arrived
and was beginning the operation SS men made their way
into the flat where it was going on, shot the anaesthetized
patient lying on the operating table, and then shot the surgeon and everyone else present.

On Wednesday, 22 July, I went into the city at about ten
in the morning. The mood in the streets was a little less tense
than the evening before. A reassuring rumour was circulating
to the effect that the Council functionaries arrested yesterday
had been set free again. So the Germans did not intend to
resettle us just yet, since in such cases (as we had heard in
reports from outside Warsaw where much smaller Jewish
communities had been resettled long ago) they always began
by liquidating the officials.

It was eleven o'clock when I came to the bridge over
Chłodna Street. I was walking along, deep in thought, and
at first I did not notice that people were standing still on the
bridge and pointing at something. Then they rapidly dis-
persed in agitation.

I was about to climb the steps to the wooden arch of the bridge when a friend I had not seen for quite a long time seized my arm.

'What are you doing here?' He was greatly agitated, and when he spoke his lower lip twitched comically, like a rabbit's muzzle. 'Go home at once!'

'What's up?'

'The action begins in an hour's time.'

'That's impossible!'

'Impossible?' He gave a bitter, nervous laugh, then turned me to face the balustrade and pointed down Chłodna Street. 'Look at that!'

A detachment of soldiers in unfamiliar yellow uniforms was marching down Chłodna Street, led by a German NCO. Every few steps the unit halted, and one of the soldiers took up his position by the wall surrounding the ghetto.

'Ukrainians. We're surrounded!' He sobbed rather than spoke these words. Then he hurried down the steps without a goodbye.

Sure enough, around noon the troops did indeed begin clearing the old people's homes, the veterans' homes and the overnight shelters. These shelters accommodated Jews from the country around Warsaw who had been thrown into the ghetto, as well as those expelled from Germany, Czecho-slovakia, Romania and Hungary. By afternoon posters had gone up in the city announcing the beginning of the resettle-ment action. All Jews fit to work were going to the east. Everyone could take twenty kilos of luggage, provisions for two days – and their jewellery. When they reached their destination those able to work would be housed in barracks and given jobs in the local German factories. Only the officials of the Jewish social institutions and the Jewish Coun-

cil were exempt. For the first time, a decree did not carry
the signature of the chairman of the Jewish Council. Czer-
niaków had killed himself by taking cyanide.

So the worst had happened after all: the people of a whole
quarter, a place with a population of half a million, were to
be resettled. It seemed absurd – no one could believe it.

During the first few days the action proceeded by the lottery
system. Buildings were surrounded at random, now in one part
of the ghetto, now in another. A whistle summoned all the
inhabitants of a house out into the yard, loaded up everyone
without exception on horse-drawn carts, regardless of sex or
age, from babies to the old, and took them to the *Umschlagplatz* – the assembly and transit centre. Then the victims were
crammed into trucks and dispatched into the unknown.

At first the action was carried out entirely by Jewish police,
led by three of the German executioners' assistants: Colonel
Szeryński, Captain Lejkin and Captain Ehrlich. They were
no less dangerous and pitiless than the Germans themselves.
Perhaps they were even worse, for when they found people
who had hidden somewhere instead of going down to the
yard they could easily be persuaded to turn a blind eye, but
only for money. Tears, pleas, even the desperate screams of
children left them unmoved.

Since the shops had been closed and the ghetto was cut
off from all supplies, hunger became widespread after a
couple of days, and this time it affected everyone. People
did not stop to let that bother them much: they were after
something more important than food. They wanted certificates of employment.

I can think of only one comparison that would give an
idea of our life in those terrible days and hours: it was like
an anthill under threat. When some thoughtless idiot's brutal

foot begins to destroy the insects' home with its hobnailed heel, the ants will scurry hither and thither, searching more and more busily for some way out, a way to save themselves, but whether because they are paralysed by the suddenness of the attack, or in concern for the fate of their offspring and whatever else they can save, they turn back as if under some baleful influence instead of going straight ahead and out of range, always returning to the same pathways and the same places, unable to break out of the deadly circle – and so they perish. Just like us.

It was a dreadful period for us, but the Germans did very good business at this time. German firms shot up in the ghetto like mushrooms after rain, and they were all ready to make out certificates of employment. For a certain number of thousands, of course, but the size of these sums did not deter people. There were queues outside such firms, assuming huge proportions outside the offices of the really large and important factories such as Toebbens and Schultz. Those who were lucky enough to have acquired certificates of employment pinned little notices to their clothing, giving the name of the place where they were supposed to be working. They thought this would protect them from resettlement.

I could easily have got hold of such a certificate, but again, as with the typhus vaccine, just for myself. None of my acquaintances, even those with the very best connections, would entertain the idea of providing certificates for my whole family. Six free certificates – that was certainly a lot to expect, but I could not afford to pay even the lowest price for all of us. I earned from one day to the next, and whatever I earned we ate. The beginning of the action in the ghetto had found me with only a few hundred złoty in my pocket. I was shattered by my helplessness, and by having to watch as my richer friends easily secured their families' safety. Unkempt, unshaven, without a morsel of food inside me, I trudged around from morning to night, from one firm to another, begging people to take pity on us. After six days of this, and pulling all the strings I could, I somehow managed to scrape the certificates together.

It must have been the week before the action began that I met Roman Kramsztyk for the last time. He was emaciated and nervous, although he tried to hide it. He was pleased to see me. 'Not off on tour yet?' he said, trying to crack a joke.

'No,' I replied briefly. I did not feel like joking. Then I asked him the question we were always putting to each other at the time. 'What do you think? Will they resettle us all?'

He did not answer my question, but avoided it by remarking, 'You look terrible!' He looked at me sympathetically. 'You take all this too much to heart.'

'How can I help it?' I shrugged my shoulders.

He smiled, lit a cigarette, said nothing for a while, and then went on, 'You wait, it'll all be over some fine day, because . . .' and he waved his arms about . . . 'because there really isn't any sense in it, is there?'

He said this with comic and rather helpless conviction, as if the utter pointlessness of what was going on was obviously an argument showing that it would end.

Unfortunately, it did not. Indeed, matters became even worse when Lithuanians and Ukrainians were brought in over the next few days. They were just as venal as the Jewish police, although in a different way. They took bribes, but as soon as they had received them they killed the people whose money they had taken. They liked killing anyway: killing for sport, or to make their work easier, as target practice or simply for fun. They killed children before their mothers' eyes and found the women's despair amusing. They shot people in the stomach to watch their torments. Sometimes several of them would line their victims up in a row and throw hand grenades at them from a distance to see who had the best aim. Every war casts up certain small groups among ethnic populations: minorities too cowardly to fight openly, too insignificant to play any independent political part, but despicable enough to act as paid executioners to one of the fighting powers. In this war those people were the Ukrainian and Lithuanian Fascists.

Roman Kramsztyk was one of the first to die when they began taking a hand in the resettlement action. The building where he lived was surrounded, but he did not go down to the yard when he heard the whistle. He preferred to be shot at home among his pictures.

At about this time the Gestapo agents Kon and Heller died. They had not established their position skilfully enough, or perhaps they were too thrifty. They only paid one of the two SS headquarters in Warsaw, and it was their bad luck to fall into the hands of men from the other. The authorizations they produced, being made out by the rival SS unit, enraged their captors even further: they were not content with simply shooting Kon and Heller, but had the dustcarts brought, and on these, amidst the refuse and filth, the two magnates took their last journey through the ghetto to a mass grave.

The Ukrainians and Lithuanians paid no attention to any certificates of employment. My six days spent acquiring ours had been a waste of effort. I felt one really had to work; the question was how to go about it. I lost heart entirely. I lay on my bed all day now, listening to the sounds coming up from the street. Every time I heard the rumble of wheels on the tarmac I panicked again. These vehicles were taking people to the *Umschlagplatz*. But they did not all pass straight through the ghetto, and any one of them could stop outside our building. We might hear the whistle in the yard any moment now. I kept jumping out of bed, going to the window, lying down again, getting up again.

I was the only one of the family to act with such shameful weakness. Perhaps it was because I alone might somehow be able to save us, through my popularity as a performer, and so I felt responsible.

My parents, sisters and brother knew there was nothing they could do. They concentrated entirely on staying in control of themselves and maintaining the fiction of ordinary daily life. Father played his violin all day, Henryk studied, Regina and Halina read and Mother mended our clothes.

The Germans hit upon yet another bright idea to ease their task. Decrees appeared on the walls stating that all families who voluntarily came to the *Umschlagplatz* to 'emigrate' would get a loaf of bread and a kilo of jam per person, and such volunteer families would not be separated. There was a massive response to this offer. People were anxious to take it up both because they were hungry and in the hope of going the unknown, difficult way to their fate together.

Unexpectedly, Goldfeder came to our aid. He had the chance to employ a certain number of people at the collection centre near the *Umschlagplatz* where the furniture and belongings from the homes of Jews who had already been resettled were sorted. He got me, my father and Henryk accommodation there, and we then succeeded in getting my sisters and mother to join us, although they did not work at the collection centre but looked after our new 'home' in the building which was our barracks. The rations were nothing special: we each got half a loaf of bread and quarter of a litre of soup a day, and we had to portion it out cleverly to satisfy our hunger as best we could.

It was my first work for the Germans. I carted furniture, mirrors, carpets, underclothes, bedclothes and clothing around from morning to night: items that had belonged to someone only a few days ago, had shown that an interior was the home of people with or without good taste, prosperous or poor, kind or cruel. Now they belonged to no one; they were downgraded into stacks and heaps of objects, they were roughly handled, and only occasionally, when I was carrying an armful of underclothes, did the faint scent of someone's favourite perfume rise from them very delicately, like a memory, or I might glimpse coloured monograms on a white background for a moment. But I had no time to think of these things. Every moment of contemplation, even of inattention, brought a painful blow or kick with a policeman's iron-tipped boot or rubber truncheon. It could cost you your life, as it did the young men who were shot on the spot because they dropped a drawing-room mirror and it broke.

Early on the morning of 2 August the order came out for all Jews to leave the small ghetto by six in the evening that day. I succeeded in getting time off to fetch some clothes and bedding from Śliska Street, along with my compositions, a collection of reviews of my performances and my creative work as a composer, and Father's violin. I took them to our barracks in a handcart, which was hard work. This was all we owned.

One day, around 5 August, when I had taken a brief rest from work and was walking down Gęsia Street, I happened to see Janusz Korczak and his orphans leaving the ghetto.

The evacuation of the Jewish orphanage run by Janusz

Korczak had been ordered for that morning. The children were to have been taken away alone. He had the chance to save himself, and it was only with difficulty that he persuaded the Germans to take him too. He had spent long years of his life with children, and now, on this last journey, he would not leave them alone. He wanted to ease things for them. He told the orphans they were going out into the country, so they ought to be cheerful. At last they would be able to exchange the horrible, suffocating city walls for meadows of flowers, streams where they could bathe, woods full of berries and mushrooms. He told them to wear their best clothes, and so they came out into the yard, two by two, nicely dressed and in a happy mood.

The little column was led by an SS man who loved children, as Germans do, even those he was about to see on their way into the next world. He took a special liking to a boy of twelve, a violinist who had his instrument under his arm. The SS man told him to go to the head of the procession of children and play – and so they set off.

When I met them in Gęsia Street the smiling children were singing in chorus, the little violinist was playing for them and Korczak was carrying two of the smallest infants, who were beaming too, and telling them some amusing story.

I am sure that even in the gas chamber, as the Cyclon B gas was stifling childish throats and striking terror instead of hope into the orphans' hearts, the Old Doctor must have whispered with one last effort, 'It's all right, children, it will be all right,' so that at least he could spare his little charges the fear of passing from life to death.

Finally, on 16 August 1942, our turn came. A selection had been carried out at the collecting centre, and only Henryk and Halina were passed as still fit to work. Father,

Regina and I were told to go back to the barracks. Once we were there the building was surrounded, and we heard the whistle in the yard.

It was no use struggling any more. I had done what I could to save my loved ones and myself. It had obviously been impossible from the start. Perhaps at least Halina and Henryk would fare better than the rest of us.

We dressed quickly, as shouts and shots were heard down in the yard, urging us to hurry. Mother packed a little bundle with anything that came to hand, and then we went down the stairs.

9 ~ The *Umschlagplatz*

The *Umschlagplatz* lay on the border of the ghetto. A compound by the railway sidings, it was surrounded by a network of dirty streets, alleys and pathways. Despite its unprepossessing appearance, it had contained riches before the war. One of the sidings had been the destination of large quantities of goods from all over the world. Jewish businessmen bargained over them, later supplying them to the Warsaw shops from depots in Nalewki Street and Simon Passage. The place was a huge oval, partly surrounded by buildings, partly fenced, with a number of roads running into it like streams into a lake, useful links with the city. The area had been closed off with gates where the streets reached it, and could now contain up to eight thousand people.

When we arrived it was still quite empty. People were walking up and down, searching in vain for water. It was a hot, fine day in late summer. The sky was blue-grey, as if it would turn to ashes in the heat rising from the trodden ground and the dazzling walls of the buildings, and the blazing sun squeezed the last drops of sweat from exhausted bodies.

At the edge of the compound, where one of the streets ran into it, there was an unoccupied space. Everyone was giving this spot a wide berth, never lingering there but casting glances of horror at it. Bodies lay there: the bodies of those killed yesterday for some crime or other, perhaps even for attempting to escape. Among the bodies of men were the corpses of a young woman and two girls with their skulls smashed to pieces. The wall under which the corpses lay showed clear traces of bloodstains and brain tissue. The children had been murdered by a favourite German method: seized by the legs, their heads swung violently against the wall. Large black flies were walking over the dead and the pools of spilt blood on the ground, and the bodies were almost visibly bloating and decaying in the heat.

We had settled down reasonably comfortably, waiting for the train. Mother was sitting on the bundle of our things, Regina was on the ground beside her, I was standing, and Father was walking nervously up and down, his hands behind his back, four steps one way, four steps back. Only now, in the glaring sunlight, when there was no point in worrying about any useless plans to save us any more, did I have time to examine Mother closely. She looked dreadful, although she was apparently fully in control of herself. Her hair, once beautiful and always carefully tended, had hardly any colour left in it and was hanging down in strands over her careworn, wrinkled face. The light in her bright black eyes seemed to have gone out, and a nervous twitch ran down from her right temple and over her cheek to the corner of her mouth. I had never noticed it before, and it showed how distressed Mother was by the scene around us. Regina was weeping, with her hands in front of her face, the tears running through her fingers.

At intervals vehicles drove up to the gates of the *Umschlagplatz* and crowds of people destined for resettlement were herded in. These new arrivals did not conceal their despair. The men were talking in raised voices, and women whose children had been taken away from them were wailing and sobbing convulsively. But soon the atmosphere of leaden apathy reigning over the compound began to affect them too. They quietened down, and only occasionally was there a brief outbreak of panic when it entered the head of a passing SS man to shoot someone who did not get out of his way quickly enough, or whose expression was not sufficiently humble.

A young woman sat on the ground not far away from us. Her dress was torn and her hair dishevelled, as if she had been fighting someone. Now, however, she sat there quite calmly, her face like death, her eyes fixed on some point in space. Her fingers spread wide, clutching her throat, and from time to time she asked, with monotonous regularity, 'Why did I do it? Why did I do it?'

A young man standing beside her, obviously her husband, was trying to comfort her and convince her of something, speaking softly, but it did not seem to penetrate her mind.

We kept meeting acquaintances among the people driven into the compound. They came over to us, greeted us, and out of sheer habit tried to make some kind of conversation, but it was not long before these conversations broke off. They moved away, preferring to try to master their anxiety alone.

The sun rose higher and higher, blazing down, and we suffered increasing torments of hunger and thirst. We had eaten the last of our bread and soup the evening before. It was difficult to stay put in one place, and I decided to walk about; that might be an improvement.

As more and more people arrived the place became increasingly crowded, and you had to avoid groups of people standing and lying around. They were all discussing the same subject: where we would be taken, and if we were really going to be sent to do labour, as the Jewish police tried to convince everyone.

I saw a group of old people lying down in one part of the compound, men and women probably evacuated from an old people's home. They were dreadfully thin, exhausted by hunger and the heat, and obviously at the very limit of their strength. Some of them were lying there with their eyes closed, and you could not tell if they were already dead or just dying. If we were going to be a labour force, then what were these old people doing here?

Women carrying children dragged themselves from group to group, begging for a drop of water. The Germans had turned off the water supply to the *Umschlagplatz* on purpose. The children's eyes were lifeless, their lids already drooping over them: their little heads nodded on thin necks, and their dry lips were open like the mouths of small fish discarded on the bank by the fishermen.

When I came back to my family they were not alone. A friend of Mother's was sitting beside her, and her husband, once the owner of a large shop, had joined my father and another acquaintance of theirs. The businessman was in quite good spirits. However, their other companion, a dentist who used to practise in Śliska Street not far from our flat, saw everything in very dark hues. He was nervous and bitter.

'It's a disgrace to us all!' he almost screamed. 'We're letting them take us to our death like sheep to the slaughter! If we attacked the Germans, half a million of us, we could break out of the ghetto, or at least die honourably, not as a stain on the face of history!'

Father listened. Rather embarrassed, but with a kindly smile, he shrugged his shoulders slightly and asked, 'How can you be absolutely certain they're sending us to our death?'

The dentist clasped his hands. 'Well, of course I don't know for certain. How could I? Are they about to tell us? But you can be ninety per cent sure they plan to wipe us all out!'

Father smiled again, as if he were even more sure of himself after this reply. 'Look,' he said, indicating the crowd at the *Umschlagplatz*. 'We're not heroes! We're perfectly ordinary people, which is why we prefer to risk hoping for that ten per cent chance of living.'

The businessman agreed with Father. His opinion too was diametrically opposite to the dentist's: the Germans couldn't be so stupid as to squander the huge potential labour force represented by the Jews. He thought we were going to labour camps, perhaps very strictly run labour camps, but surely they would not kill us.

Meanwhile the businessman's wife was telling Mother and Regina how she had left her silverware walled up in the cellar. It was beautiful, valuable silver, and she expected to find it again on her return from deportation.

It was already afternoon when we saw a new group for resettlement being herded into the compound. We were horrified to see Halina and Henryk among them. So they were to share our fate too – and it had been such a comfort to think that at least the two of them would be safe.

I hurried to meet Henryk, certain that his idiotically upright attitude was to blame for bringing him and Halina here. I bombarded him with questions and reproaches before he could get a word of explanation in, but he was not going to deign to answer me anyway. He shrugged his shoulders, took a small Oxford edition of Shakespeare out of his pocket, moved over to one side of us and began to read.

It was Halina who told us what had happened. They heard at work that we had been taken away, and they simply volunteered to go to the *Umschlagplatz* because they wanted to be with us.

What a stupid emotional reaction on their part! I decided to get them away from here at any price. After all, they were not on the list for resettlement. They could stay in Warsaw.

The Jewish policeman who had brought them knew me from the Sztuka café, and I was counting on being able to soften his heart quite easily, particularly as there was no formal reason for the two of them to be here. Unfortunately I had miscalculated: he wouldn't hear of letting them go. Like every policeman, he was duty bound to deliver five people to the *Umschlagplatz* every day personally, on pain of being resettled himself if he did not comply. Halina and Henryk made up today's quota of five. He was tired and had no intention of letting them go and setting out to chase up two more people, God knew where. In his opinion these hunts were not an easy assignment, since people would not come when the police called them but hid instead, and anyway he was sick of the whole thing.

I went back to my family empty-handed. Even this last attempt to save at least a couple of us had failed, like all my earlier attempts. I sat down beside Mother in a very downcast mood.

It was now five in the afternoon, but as hot as ever, and the crowd grew greater with every passing hour. People got lost in the crush and called to one another in vain. We heard the shots and shouting which meant raids were going on in the nearby streets. Agitation grew as the hour approached at which the train was supposed to come.

The woman next to us who kept asking, 'Why did I do it?' got on our nerves more than anyone else. We knew what she was talking about by now. Our friend the businessman had found out. When everyone was told to leave their building this woman, her husband and their child had hidden in a place prepared in advance. As the police were passing it the baby began crying, and in her fear the mother smothered it with her own hands. Unfortunately even that did not help. The baby's crying and then its death rattle were heard, and the hiding place was discovered.

At one point a boy made his way through the crowd in our direction with a box of sweets on a string round his neck. He was selling them at ridiculous prices, although heaven knows what he thought he was going to do with the money. Scraping together the last of our small change, we bought a single cream caramel. Father divided it into six parts with his penknife. That was our last meal together.

Around six o'clock a sense of nervous tension came over the compound. Several German cars had driven up, and the police were inspecting those destined to be taken away, picking out the young and strong. These lucky ones were obviously to be used for other purposes. A crowd of many thousands began pressing that way; people were shouting, trying to drown each other out, get to the front and display their physical advantages. The Germans responded by firing. The dentist, still with our group, could scarcely contain his indignation. He snapped furiously at my father, as if it were all his fault. 'So now do you believe me when I say they're going to kill us all? People fit for work will stay here. Death lies that way!'

His voice broke as he tried to shout this above the noise of the crowd and the shooting, pointing the way the transports were to go.

Downcast and grief-stricken, Father did not reply. The businessman shrugged his shoulders and smiled ironically; he was still in good spirits. He did not think the selection of a few hundred people meant anything.

The Germans had finally picked their labour force and now drove off, but the crowd's agitation did not die down. Soon afterwards we heard the whistle of a locomotive in the distance and the sound of trucks rattling over the rails as they came closer. A few more minutes, and the train came into sight: more than a dozen cattle trucks and goods trucks rolling slowly towards us. The evening breeze, blowing in the same direction, wafted a suffocating wave of chlorine our way.

At the same time the cordon of Jewish police and SS men surrounding the compound became denser and began making its way towards its centre. Once again we heard shots fired to frighten us. Loud wailing from the women and the sound of children weeping rose from the close-packed crowd.

We got ready to leave. Why wait? The sooner we were in the trucks the better. A line of police was stationed a few paces away from the train, leaving a broad path open for the crowd. The path led to the open doors of the chlorinated trucks.

By the time we had made our way to the train the first trucks were already full. People were standing in them pressed close to each other. SS men were still pushing with their rifle butts, although there were loud cries from inside and complaints about the lack of air. And indeed the smell of chlorine made breathing difficult, even some distance from the trucks. What went on in there if the floors had to be so heavily chlorinated? We had gone about halfway down the train when I suddenly heard someone shout, 'Here! Here, Szpilman!' A hand grabbed me by the collar, and I was flung back and out of the police cordon.

Who dared do such a thing? I didn't want to be parted from my family. I wanted to stay with them!

My view was now of the closed ranks of the policemen's backs. I threw myself against them, but they did not give way. Peering past the policemen's heads I could see Mother and Regina, helped by Halina and Henryk, clambering into the trucks, while Father was looking around for me.

'Papa!' I shouted.

He saw me and took a couple of steps my way, but then hesitated and stopped. He was pale, and his lips trembled nervously. He tried to smile, helplessly, painfully, raised his hand and waved goodbye, as if I were setting out into life and he was already greeting me from beyond the grave. Then he turned and went towards the trucks.

I flung myself at the policemen's shoulders again with all my might.

'Papa! Henryk! Halina!'

I shouted like someone possessed, terrified to think that now, at the last vital moment, I might not get to them and we would be parted for ever.

One of the policemen turned and looked angrily at me.

'What the hell do you think you're doing? Go on, save yourself!'

Save myself? From what? In a flash I realized what awaited the people in the cattle trucks. My hair stood on end. I glanced behind me. I saw the open compound, the railway lines and platforms, and beyond them the streets. Driven by compulsive animal fear, I ran for the streets, slipped in among a column of Council workers just leaving the place, and got through the gate that way.

When I could think straight again, I was on a pavement among buildings. An SS man came out of one of the houses with a Jewish policeman. The SS man had an impassive, arrogant face; the policeman was positively crawling to him, smiling, dancing attendance. He pointed to the train standing at the *Umschlagplatz* and said to the German, with comradely familiarity and in a sarcastic tone, 'Well, off they go for meltdown!'

I looked the way he was pointing. The doors of the trucks had been closed, and the train was starting off, slowly and laboriously.

I turned away and staggered down the empty street, weeping out loud, pursued by the fading cries of the people shut up in those trucks. It sounded like the twittering of caged birds in deadly peril.

10 ~ A Chance of Life

I simply walked straight ahead. I didn't mind where I went. The *Umschlagplatz* and the trucks carrying my family away were behind me now. I could not hear the train any longer; it was already several kilometres beyond the city. Yet I could feel it inside me as it moved away. With every step I took along the pavement I became lonelier. I was aware of being torn irrevocably from everything that had made up my life until now. I did not know what awaited me, only that it was sure to be as bad as I could imagine. There was no way I could return to the building where our family had last been living. The SS guards would kill me on the spot, or send me back to the *Umschlagplatz* as someone left off the resettlement transport by mistake. I had no idea where I would spend the night, but at the moment I did not really care, although there was a lurking fear of the coming twilight in my unconscious mind.

The street might have been swept clean: doors were locked or left wide open in the buildings from which all the inhabitants had been taken. A Jewish policeman approached me. I was not interested in him, and would have paid him no attention if he had not stopped and cried out, 'Władek!'

When I too stopped, he added in surprise, 'What are you doing here at this time of day?'

It was only now that I recognized him. He was a relation of mine, and not popular in our family. We thought his morals

dubious and tried to avoid him. He could always wriggle out
of difficulty somehow, and he kept falling on his feet by dint
of methods other people would regard as wrong. When he
joined the police it merely confirmed his bad reputation.

As soon as I recognized him in his uniform all these
thoughts went through my head, but next moment it occurred
to me that he was now my closest relation, in fact my only
relation. Anyway, here was someone connected with the
memory of my family.

'It's like this . . .' I began. I was going to tell him how my
parents, my brother and my sisters had been taken away,
but I could not get another word out. However, he understood. He came up to me and took my arm.

'Perhaps it's better that way,' he whispered, and made a
gesture of resignation. 'The quicker the better, really. It's
waiting for us all.' After a moment's silence, he added, 'Anyway, come round to our place. It will cheer us all up a bit.'

I agreed, and spent my first night on my own with these
relations.

In the morning I went to see Mieczysław Lichtenbaum,
the son of the new chairman of the Jewish Council, whom I
had known well when I was still playing the piano in the
ghetto cafés. He suggested that I could play in the German
extermination commando's casino, where the Gestapo and
SS officers relaxed in the evening after a tiring day spent
murdering Jews. They were served by Jews who would
sooner or later be murdered too. Of course I did not want to
accept such an offer, although Lichtenbaum couldn't understand why it did not appeal to me, and was hurt when I
declined. Without further discussion, he got me enrolled in a
column of workers demolishing the walls of the former large
ghetto, now to be incorporated with the Aryan part of the city.

Next day I left the Jewish quarter for the first time in two years. It was a fine, hot day, somewhere around 20 August. Just as fine as it had been for many days before, as fine as the last day I spent with my family at the *Umschlagplatz*. We walked in a column in rows of four abreast, under the command of Jewish foremen, guarded by two SS men. We stopped in Żelazna Brama Square. So there was still life like this somewhere!

Street traders with baskets full of wares stood outside the market hall, now closed and presumably converted into some sort of stores by the Germans. Gleaming sunlight brought a glow to the colours of fruit and vegetables, made the scales of the fish sparkle, and struck dazzling light from the tin lids of preserve jars. Women were walking around the traders, bargaining, going from basket to basket, making their purchases and then moving off towards the city centre. The dealers in gold and currency were calling out monotonously, 'Gold, buy gold. Dollars, roubles!'

At some point a vehicle hooted far down a side street, and the grey-green shape of a police truck came into sight. The traders panicked, hastily packed up their wares and fell over themselves in their efforts to get away. There was shouting and hopeless confusion all over the square. So even here everything was not really all right!

We were trying to work as slowly as possible on the demolition of the wall, so that the job would last a long time. The Jewish foremen did not harrass us, and even the SS men did not behave as badly here as inside the ghetto. They stood a little way off, deep in conversation, letting their eyes wander.

The truck passed the square and disappeared. The traders went back to their previous positions, and the square looked as if nothing had happened. My companions left our group

one by one to buy things at the stalls and stow them in bags
they had brought, or up their trouser legs and in their jackets.
Unfortunately I had no money and could only watch,
although I felt faint with hunger.

A young couple approached our group, coming from
Ogród Saski. They were both very well dressed. The young
woman looked charming; I couldn't tear my eyes away from
her. Her painted mouth was smiling, she swayed slightly
from the hips, and the sun turned her fair hair to gold in a
shimmering halo around her head. As she passed us the
young woman slowed her pace, crying, 'Look – oh, do look!'

The man did not understand. He looked enquiringly at
her.

She pointed at us. 'Jews!'

He was surprised. 'So?' He shrugged his shoulders. 'Are
those the first Jews you've ever seen?'

The woman smiled in some embarrassment, pressed close
to her companion, and they went on their way in the direction
of the market.

That afternoon I managed to borrow fifty złoty from one
of the others. I spent it on bread and potatoes. I ate some
of the bread and took the rest of it and the potatoes back
to the ghetto. I did the first commercial deal of my life that
evening. I had paid twenty złoty for the bread; I sold it for
fifty in the ghetto. The potatoes had cost three złoty a kilo;
I sold them for eighteen. I had enough to eat for the first
time in ages, and a little working capital still in hand to make
my purchases next day.

The demolition work was very monotonous. We left the
ghetto early in the morning and then stood around a heap
of bricks looking as if we were working until five in the
afternoon. My companions passed the time by engaging in

all kinds of transactions as they acquired goods and specu-
lated on what to buy, how to smuggle it into the ghetto and
how to sell it most profitably there. I bought the simplest
things, just enough to earn my keep. If I thought of anything
it was of my family: where they were now, what camp they
had been taken to, how they were getting on there.

One day an old friend of mine passed our group. He was
Tadeusz Blumental, a Jew, but one whose features were so
'Aryan' that he did not have to admit his origins and could
live outside the ghetto walls. He was glad to see me, but
distressed to find me in such a difficult situation. He gave
me some money and promised to try to help me. He said a
woman would come next day, and if I could slip away
unobserved she would take me to a place where I could hide.
The woman did come, but unfortunately with the news that
the people with whom I was to have stayed would not agree
to take in a Jew.

Another day the leader of the Warsaw Philharmonic, Jan
Dworakowski, saw me as he was crossing the square. He was
genuinely moved to see me. He embraced me and began
asking how I and my family were. When I told him that the
others had been taken away from Warsaw he looked at me
with what struck me as particular sympathy, and opened his
mouth as if to say something. But at the last minute he did
not.

'What do you think will have happened to them?' I asked
in great anxiety.

'Władysław!' He took my hands and pressed them warmly.
'Perhaps it's best for you to know . . . so you can be on your
guard.' He hesitated for a moment, pressed my hand, and
then added quietly, almost in a whisper, 'You'll never see
them again.'

He turned quickly and hurried away. After a couple of paces he turned again and came back to embrace me, but I was not strong enough to return his cordiality. Subconsciously, I had known from the first that the German fairy-tales of camps for Jews where 'good working conditions' awaited them on resettlement were lies – that we could expect only death at the hands of the Germans. Yet like the other Jews in the ghetto, I had cherished the illusion that it could be different, that this time German promises meant what they said. When I thought of my family I tried to imagine them alive, even if they were living in terrible conditions, but alive anyway: then we might see each other again some day after all. Dworakowski had destroyed the structure of self-deception I had so arduously maintained. Only much later could I convince myself that he had been right to do so: the certainty of death gave me the energy to save myself at the crucial moment.

I spent the next few days as if in a dream, automatically getting up in the morning, automatically moving about, lying down automatically in the evening to sleep on a plank bed in the Jewish furniture warehouse that had been assigned to the Council. Somehow or other I had to come to terms with what I now knew was the certain death of Mother, Father, Halina, Regina and Henryk. There was a Soviet air raid on Warsaw. Everyone went into the bunkers. The Germans were alarmed and angry, the Jews delighted, although they could not show it. Every time we heard the drone of bombers our faces lit up; to us, they were the sound of approaching aid and the defeat of Germany, the only thing that could save us. I did not go down into a bunker – it was all the same to me whether I lived or died.

Meanwhile our working conditions as we demolished the

walls had deteriorated. The Lithuanians now guarding us made sure we bought nothing in the market, and we were inspected more and more thoroughly at the main guard station and on our return to the ghetto. One afternoon, quite unexpectedly, a selection was made in our group. A young policeman stationed himself outside the main guard station with his sleeves rolled up and began dividing us up according to the lottery system, just as he thought best: those on the left to die, those on the right to live. He ordered me over to the right. Those on the left had to lie face-down on the ground. Then he shot them with his revolver.

After about a week announcements of a new selection from all the Jews left in Warsaw were pasted on the ghetto walls. Three hundred thousand had already been 'resettled'; about a hundred thousand were now left, and only twenty-five thousand of these were to remain in the city, all of them professional people and other workers indispensable to the Germans.

The Council functionaries had to go to the yard of the Jewish Council building on the appointed day, the rest of the population to the section of the ghetto between Nowolipki and Gęsia Streets. To make matters doubly sure, one of the Jewish policemen, an officer called Blaupapier, stood in front of the Council building with a whip in his hand, personally using it on anyone who tried to get in.

Numbers stamped on bits of paper were handed out to those who were to stay in the ghetto. The Council had a right to keep five thousand of its own officials. I was not given a number that first day, but none the less I slept all night, resigned to my fate, although my companions were almost out of their minds with anxiety. Next morning I did get a number. We were stationed in rows, four abreast, and had to wait until the SS control commission under Unter-sturmführer Brandt condescended to come and count us, in case too many of us might be going to escape death.

Four by four, marching in step and surrounded by police, we made for the gate of the Council building to go to Gęsia Street, where we were to be lodged. Behind us, the crowd of people condemned to death flung themselves about, screaming, wailing and cursing us for our own miraculous escape, while the Lithuanians who were supervising their passage from life to death shot into the crowd to calm it in what was now their usual manner.

So I had been given a chance to live yet again. But to live how long?

11 ~ 'Marksmen arise!'

I had moved house once more, the latest of I don't know how many moves since we were living in Śliska Street and the war broke out. This time we were given shared rooms, or rather cells containing only the most essential household equipment and plank beds. Mine was shared with the three members of the Próżański family and Mrs A, a silent lady who kept herself to herself, although she had to do so in the same room as the rest of us. The very first night there I had a dream that utterly discouraged me. It seemed to be final confirmation of my assumptions about the fate of my family. I dreamed of my brother Henryk, who came up to me, leaned over my bed and said, 'We are dead now.'

We were woken at six in the morning by much coming and going in the passage outside. There was loud talk and a lot of activity. The privileged labourers working on the conversion of the Warsaw SS commandant's palace in Aleje Ujazdowskie were off to work. Their 'privileged' status meant that they were given nourishing soup with meat in it before they set out; it was satisfying, and the effects would last some hours. We went out soon after them, our bellies almost empty after some watery broth. Its poor nutritional value matched the importance of our work: we were to clean the yard of the Jewish Council building.

Next day they sent me, Próżański and his half-grown son

to the building which housed the Council storerooms and the flats of Council functionaries. It was two in the afternoon when the familiar German whistle and the customary German yell were heard summoning everyone to the yard. Although we had already suffered so much at the hands of the Germans we froze like pillars of salt. Only two days ago we had been allotted the numbers that meant life. Everyone in this building had one, so surely this could not be another selection. In which case, what was it? We hurried down: yes, it really was a selection. Yet again I saw people cast into despair and listened to the SS men shouting and fuming as they tore families apart and sorted us to right and left, cursing and beating us. Once more, our working group was destined to live, with a few exceptions. Among the exceptions was Próżański's son, a delightful boy with whom I had made friends. I had already grown very fond of him, even though we had been living in the same room for only two days. I will not describe his parents' despair. Thousands of other mothers and fathers in the ghetto were equally desperate during those months. There was an even more characteristic aspect to the selection: the families of prominent personalities in the Jewish community bought their freedom from the supposedly incorruptible Gestapo officers on the spot. To make up the correct numbers carpenters, waiters, hairdressers and barbers and other skilled workers who really could have been useful to the Germans were sent to the *Umschlagplatz* instead, and taken away to their deaths. Incidentally, young Próżański escaped from the *Umschlagplatz* and thus survived a little longer.

One day soon afterwards our group leader told me he had succeeded in getting me assigned to the group working on the building of the SS barracks in the remote Mokotow district. I would get better food and be much better off in general there, he assured me.

The reality was very different. I had to get up two hours earlier and walk about a dozen kilometres through the middle of the city to get to work on time. When I arrived, exhausted from my long trek, I had to get straight down to labour which was far beyond my strength, carrying bricks stacked on top of each other on a board on my back. In between times I carried buckets of lime and iron bars. I might have done all right but for the SS overseers, the future occupants of this barracks, who thought we were working too slowly. They ordered us to carry the piles of bricks or iron bars at a run, and if anyone felt faint and stopped they beat him with hide whips that had balls of lead set into the leather.

In fact, I don't know how I would have coped with this first bout of hard physical labour if I had not gone to the group leader again and pleaded, successfully, to be transferred to the group building the SS commander's little palace in Aleje Ujazdowskie. Conditions were more tolerable there, and I managed somehow. They were tolerable chiefly because we were working with German master masons and skilled Polish artisans, some of whom were forced labour, although some were working on contract. As a consequence, we were less conspicuous and could take turns to have a break now that we were not always an obviously self-contained Jewish group. Moreover, the Poles made common cause with us against the German overseers and gave us a hand. Another helpful factor was that the architect in charge of the building was himself a Jew, an engineer called Blum, with a staff of other Jewish engineers under him, all outstanding professionals. The Germans did not officially recognize this situation, and the master mason Schultke, described for form's sake as architect-in-charge and a typical sadist, had the right to beat the engineers as often as he liked. But without the skilled Jewish artisans nothing would really have been achieved. Because of this we were all treated relatively gently – apart from the beatings mentioned above, of course, but such things hardly counted in the climate of the times.

I was hod carrier to a mason called Bartczak, a Pole and a decent fellow at heart, although of course there was bound to be some friction between us. Sometimes the Germans breathed down our necks, and we had to try working the way they wanted. I did my best, but inevitably I would tip the ladder over, spill the lime, or push bricks off the scaffolding, and Bartczak was told off too. He would be angry with me in turn, going scarlet in the face, muttering to himself and waiting for the Germans to go away, when he would push his cap back from his forehead, put his hands on his hips, shake his head over my clumsiness as a mason, and begin his tirade:

'How do you mean, you used to play music on the radio, Szpilman?' he marvelled. 'A musician like you – can't even handle a shovel and scrape lime off a board – you must have sent them all to sleep!'

He would then shrug his shoulders, look suspiciously at me, spit, and venting his anger one last time would shout at the top of his voice, 'Idiot!'

However, when I had fallen into gloomy contemplation of my own affairs and stopped work, forgetting where I was, Bartczak never failed to warn me in time if a German overseer was on his way.

'Mortar!' he would bellow, the word echoing over the site, and I would snatch up the first bucket that came to hand, or a brick trowel, and pretend to be working industriously.

The prospect of winter, which was nearly on us now, caused me particular anxiety. I had no warm clothes to wear, and of course no gloves. I have always been rather sensitive to the cold, and if my hands were frostbitten while I was doing such heavy physical labour I could write off any future career as a pianist. With mounting gloom, I watched the leaves on the trees in Aleje Ujazdowskie turn colour, as the wind blew colder day by day.

At this point the numbers which had meant provisional permission to live were given permanent status, and at the same time I was moved to new quarters in the ghetto, in Kurza Street. Our place of work was also changed, to the Aryan side of the city. Work on the little palace in the Aleje was coming to an end, and fewer workers were needed now. Some of us were transferred to 8 Narbutt Street to prepare accommodation for a unit of SS officers.

It was getting colder and colder, and my fingers went numb more and more frequently as I worked. I don't know how it would have ended if chance had not come to my aid – a lucky stroke of bad luck, so to speak. One day I stumbled carrying lime and sprained my ankle. I was now useless for work on the building site, and Blum the engineer assigned me to the stores. This was the end of November and the very last moment when I could hope to save my hands. In any case it was warmer in the stores than out of doors.

More and more labourers who had been working in Aleje Ujazdowskie were now transferred to us – and more and more of the SS men who had been our overseers there were moved to the Narbutt Street site too. One morning we found among them the man who was the bane of our lives: a sadist whose surname we did not know, but we had called him

Thwick-Thwack. He took an almost erotic pleasure in mistreating people in a certain way: he would order the delinquent to bend over, put the man's head between his thighs, press hard, and thrash the unfortunate man's behind with a kourbash, pale with fury and hissing through clenched teeth, 'Thwick-thwack, thwick-thwack.' He never let his victim go until the man had fainted with pain.

Once again rumours of further 'resettlement' were circulating in the ghetto. If they were true, it was clear that the Germans meant to exterminate us utterly. After all, there were only some sixty thousand of us left, and for what other purpose could they intend to remove this small number from the city? The idea of offering resistance to the Germans was broached with increasing frequency. Young Jewish men were particularly determined to fight, and here and there a start was made on secretly fortifying buildings in the ghetto so that they could be defended from inside if the worst happened. Obviously the Germans had got wind of these developments, for decrees went up on the ghetto walls assuring us warmly that there was not going to be any further resettlement. The men guarding our group volunteered the same information every day, and to make their assurances even more convincing they officially allowed us to buy five kilos of potatoes and a loaf of bread apiece on the Aryan side from now on, and bring them back into the ghetto. The benevolence of the Germans even persuaded them to allow a delegate from our group to move freely about the city every day and make these purchases on our behalf. We chose a brave young man known as 'Majorek', little major. The Germans had no idea that Majorek, following our instructions, would become a link between the underground resistance movement in the ghetto and similar Polish organizations outside.

Our official permission to bring a certain amount of food into the ghetto set off some busy trading around our group. There would be a crowd of dealers waiting every day when we left the ghetto. They bartered *ciuchy*, second-hand clothes, with my companions in exchange for food. I was less interested in this trade than in the news the dealers brought us at the same time. The Allies had landed in Africa. Stalingrad was now in the third month of its defence, and there had been a conspiracy in Warsaw: grenades were thrown into the German Café-Club. Each of these items of news raised our spirits, strengthening our powers of endurance and our belief that Germany would be defeated in the near future. Very soon the first armed reprisals began in the ghetto, first of all against the corrupt elements among ourselves. One of the worst of the Jewish police was murdered: Lejkin, notorious for his industry in hunting people down and delivering his quotas to the *Umschlagplatz*. Soon after him a man called First, who acted as liaison between the Gestapo and the Jewish Council, died at the hands of Jewish assassins. For the first time the spies in the ghetto began to feel afraid.

Gradually I recovered my spirits and my will to survive. I went to Majorek one day and asked him to phone some acquaintances of mine when he was in the city, and ask if they would get me out of the ghetto somehow and hide me. That afternoon I waited with a thudding heart for Majorek's return. He came back, but with bad news: my acquaintances had said they could not risk hiding a Jew. After all, they explained, rather indignant at my even having suggested such a thing, doing so carried the death penalty! Well, there was no help for it. They had said no; perhaps others would be more humane. I must not on any account give up hope.

The New Year was upon us. On 31 December 1942 a large convoy carrying coal unexpectedly arrived. We had to unload it all the same day and store it in the cellar of the building in Narbutt Street. It was hard, heavy work and took longer than expected. Instead of setting off for the ghetto at six in the evening, we did not leave until it was almost night.

We always went the same way, walking in groups of three from Polna Street to Chałubiński Street and then on along Żelazna Street to the ghetto. We had already reached Chałubiński Street, when frantic cries were heard at the head of the column. We stopped. Next moment we saw what had happened. By pure chance we had come upon two SS men, drunk as lords. One of them was Thwick-Thwack. They fell on us, beating us with the whips from which they did not part company even on a drunken spree. They did it systematically, beating each group of three in turn, beginning at the head of the column. When they had finished, they stationed themselves a few paces away on the pavement, drew their pistols, and Thwick-Thwack shouted, 'Intellectuals, fall out!'

There was no doubt of their intentions: they were going to kill us on the spot. I found it difficult to decide what to do. Failing to fall out might infuriate them even more. They could end up dragging us out of the column themselves to give us another beating before they killed us, as a punishment for failing to fall out voluntarily. The historian Dr Zajczyk, a university lecturer who was standing next to me, was trembling all over, just like me, and like me he could not make up his mind. But on the second shouted order we fell out of the column. There were seven of us in all. I found myself face to face with Thwick-Thwack again, and he was shouting at me personally now.

'I'll soon teach you discipline! What made you take so

long about it?' He waved his pistol about under my nose. 'You were supposed to be here at six, and it's ten o'clock now!'

I said nothing, sure that he was going to shoot me next moment anyway. He looked straight at me with cloudy eyes, staggered about under the street-lamp, and then unexpectedly announced in a perfectly steady voice, 'You seven are personally responsible for marching the column back to the ghetto. You can go.'

We had already turned away when he suddenly bellowed, 'Come back!'

This time he had Dr Zajczyk right in front of him. He seized him by the collar, shook him, and snarled, 'Know why we beat you?'

The doctor said nothing.

'Well, do you know why?' he repeated.

A man standing rather further off, obviously alarmed, asked timidly, 'Why?'

'To remind you it's New Year!'

When we had re-formed the column we heard a further order: 'Sing!'

Surprised, we stared at Thwick-Thwack. He tottered again, belched, and added, 'Sing something cheerful!'

Laughing at his own joke, he turned and staggered down the street. After a few paces he stopped and called out threateningly, 'And sing it good and loud!'

I don't know who was the first to strike up the tune, or why this particular soldier's song came into his head. We joined in. After all, it hardly mattered what we sang.

Only today, looking back at that incident, do I realize how much tragedy was mingled with its ridiculous aspect. That New Year's Eve a small group of utterly exhausted Jews walked through the streets of a city where declarations of Polish patriotism had been forbidden for years on pain of death, singing at the top of our voices and with total impunity the patriotic song, '*Hej, strzelcy wraz!*' – 'Hey, marksmen, arise!'

12 ~ Majorek

January the first, 1943. The year in which Roosevelt had announced that the Germans would be defeated. And indeed they were clearly less successful on the front lines now. If only the front lines had been closer to us! News of the German defeat at Stalingrad arrived; it was too important a piece of news to be hushed up or easily dismissed with the usual press claim that even this was 'of no significance for the victorious course of the war'. This time the Germans had to admit to it, and they announced three days of mourning, the first free time we had enjoyed for months. The more optimistic among us rubbed their hands with glee, firmly convinced that the war would soon be over. The pessimists thought otherwise: they believed the war would last for some time yet, but at least there could no longer be the slightest doubt of its ultimate outcome.

In parallel to the increasingly good political news, the ghetto underground organizations stepped up their activities. My group was involved too. Majorek, who delivered sacks of potatoes to our group from the city daily, smuggled in ammunition underneath the potatoes. We shared it out between us and brought it into the ghetto hidden up our trouser legs. This was a risky business, and one day it nearly ended tragically for all of us.

Majorek had delivered the sacks to my storehouse as usual. I was to empty them, hide the ammunition, and divide it out among my colleagues that evening. But no sooner had Majorek put down the sacks and left the storehouse than the door was flung open and Untersturmführer Young burst in. He looked round, noticed the sacks and marched up to them. I felt weak at the knees. If he inspected their contents we were done for, and I would be the first to get a bullet in the head. Young stopped in front of the sacks and tried to untie one. However, the string had become entangled, and it was difficult to undo it. The SS man cursed impatiently and looked at me.

'Undo that!' he snapped.

I went over to him, trying to calm my nerves. I untangled the knot with intentional slowness, apparently quite calm. Hands on his hips, the German watched.

'What's inside it?' he asked.

'Potatoes. We're allowed to bring some back to the ghetto every day.'

The sack was now open. His next order came. 'Take them out and let me see.'

I put my hand into the sack. No potatoes. As luck would have it, Majorek had bought a small amount of oatmeal and beans today instead of some of the potatoes. They were on top and the potatoes were underneath. I displayed a handful of fairly long yellow beans.

'Potatoes, eh?' Young laughed sarcastically. Then he ordered, 'Try further down!'

This time I brought up a handful of oatmeal. Any moment now the German would beat me for deceiving him. In fact I hoped he would; it might take his mind off the rest of the contents of the sack. However, he did not even slap me. He turned on his heel and left. Soon afterwards he burst in again, as if he expected to catch me committing some new offence.

I was standing in the middle of the storeroom, trying to recover from my fright. I had to pull myself together. Only when I heard Young's steps growing less distinct as he went down the passage, until at last they died away, did I hurriedly empty the sacks, hiding the ammunition under a heap of lime that had been tipped out in one corner of the storeroom. As we approached the ghetto wall that evening we threw our new consignment of bullets and hand grenades over as usual. We had got away with it!

On 14 January, a Friday, in their fury at the front-line defeats and the delight they very clearly gave the Poles, the Germans began human-hunting again. This time their hunts ranged all over Warsaw. They went on for three days without stopping. Every day, as we went to work and as we came back, we saw people being pursued and captured in the streets. Convoys of police trucks loaded with prisoners moved towards the gaol and came back empty, ready to pick up more batches of future concentration camp inmates. A number of Aryans sought refuge in the ghetto. These difficult days saw another paradox of the occupation period: the armband with the Star of David, once the most threatening of symbols, became protection overnight, a form of insurance, since Jews were no longer the quarry.

After two days, however, our own turn came. When I left the building on Monday morning I did not find the whole of our group out in the road, only a few workers obviously regarded as indispensable. As 'storeroom manager' I was among them. We set out, escorted by two policemen, in the direction of the ghetto gate. It was usually guarded only by Jewish police officers, but today a whole German police unit was carefully checking the papers of anyone leaving the ghetto to go to work. A boy of about ten came running along the pavement. He was very pale, and so scared that he forgot to take his cap off to a German policeman coming towards him. The German stopped, drew his revolver without a word, put it to the boy's temple and shot. The child fell to the ground, his arms flailing, went rigid and died. The policeman calmly put the revolver back in its holster and went on his way. I looked at him; he did not even have particularly brutal features, nor did he appear angry. He was a normal, placid man who had carried out one of his many minor daily duties and put it out of his mind again at once, for other and more important business awaited him.

Our group was already on the Aryan side when we heard shots behind us. They came from the other groups of Jewish workers, surrounded in the ghetto and answering the German terror with return fire for the first time.

We went on our way to work in downcast mood, all of us wondering what would happen in the ghetto now. There could be no doubt that a new phase of its liquidation had begun. Little Próżański was walking beside me, anxious about his parents who had stayed behind in our room, wondering whether they would manage to hide somewhere in time to escape resettlement. I had my own worries, and they were of a very specific nature: I had left my fountain pen and my watch, all I owned in the world, lying on the table in our room. If I succeeded in escaping I had planned to turn them into cash and live on the money for a few days, long enough to find somewhere to hide with the help of my friends.

We did not go back to the ghetto that evening; we were provisionally billeted in Narbutt Street. Only later did we find out what had happened behind the walls, where the people defended themselves as best they could before they were taken away to their deaths. They hid in places prepared in advance, and the women poured water on the steps of the stairways so that it would freeze and make it more difficult for the Germans to reach the upper storeys. Some of the buildings were simply barricaded and the inhabitants exchanged fire with the SS, determined to die fighting, with weapons in their hands, rather than perish in the gas chamber. The Germans had evacuated the patients in the Jewish hospital in their underwear, loaded them into open trucks in the freezing cold, and taken them off to Treblinka. But thanks to this first show of Jewish resistance the Germans took away only some five thousand people in the course of five days, instead of the ten thousand they had planned to transport.

On the fifth evening Thwick-Thwack informed us that the action to 'cleanse the ghetto of non-working elements' had been concluded, and we could go back in again. Our hearts were pounding. The streets of the ghetto were a shattering sight. Pavements were covered with glass from broken windows. The feathers of slashed pillows clogged the gutter; there were feathers everywhere; every breath of wind raised great clouds of them, eddying in the air like a thick snowfall in reverse, going from earth to sky. Every few paces we saw the bodies of murdered people. There was such silence all around that our footsteps echoed back from the walls of the buildings as if we were passing through a rocky ravine in the mountains. We found no one left in our room, but it had not been looted. Everything was just as Próżański's parents, marked down for the transports, had left it. The plank beds were still unmade from their last night there, and a pot of coffee they had not been able to finish stood on the cold stove. My fountain pen and watch were on the table where I had left them.

Now I had to act energetically and in great haste. Presum-

ably the next resettlement operation would come very soon,
and this time I might be among those listed to go. Through
Majorek I got in touch with friends, a young married artistic
couple. Andrzej Bogucki was an actor, and his wife was a
singer who performed under her maiden name of Janina
Godlewska. One day Majorek told me they would be coming
about six in the evening. At the moment when the Aryan
workers went home I seized my chance to slip out of the
gate. They were both there. We exchanged only a few words.
I handed them my compositions, my fountain pen and my
watch, everything I wanted to take with me. I had already
brought these things out of the ghetto and hidden them in
the storeroom. We agreed that Bogucki would come for me
at five o'clock on Saturday, when an SS general was to inspect
the building. I was counting on the fuss that would cause to
make it easier for me to get away.

By now the atmosphere in the ghetto had become increasingly tense and uneasy. There was a feeling of foreboding in
the air. The Jewish police commander, Colonel Szeryński,
committed suicide. He must have received some very bad
news indeed if even he, closer than anyone to the Germans,
the man they most urgently needed and who would anyway
have been the very last for resettlement, could see no way
out but death. Other Jews mingled with us daily as we went
out to work, trying to escape to the Aryan side of the wall.
They did not always succeed. There were spies over there
waiting for the fugitives, and paid agents and willing volun-
teers who would later attack the Jew they had been observing
in some side street, making him hand over any money and
jewellery he had on him and threatening to turn him in to
the Germans. Then they quite often handed the people they
had robbed over to the Germans anyway.

That Saturday I was faint with nerves from early in the morning onwards. Would it work? Any false step could mean instant death. In the afternoon the general duly turned up to make his inspection. The SS men, fully occupied, took their minds off us for the time being. Around five the Aryan workers stopped work for the day. I put my coat on, took off the armband with the blue star for the first time in three years, and slipped out of the gate with them.

Bogucki was standing on the corner of Wiśniowa Street. That meant everything had gone to plan so far. When he saw me he began moving off rapidly. I walked a few paces behind him, my coat collar turned up, trying not to lose sight of him in the dark. The streets were empty, and only dimly lit to comply with the regulations in force since the outbreak of war. I merely had to be careful I did not meet a German in the light of a street-lamp, where he might be able to see my face. We took the shortest way, walking very fast, but it still seemed endless. Finally, however, we reached our journey's end – number 10 Noakowski Street – where I was to hide on the fifth floor in an artist's studio which was at the disposal of Piotr Perkowski, one of the leaders of the musicians conspiring against the Germans at this time. We hurried up the stairs, taking them three at a time. Janina Godlewska was waiting for us in the studio; she looked nervous and fearful. On seeing us, she breathed a sigh of relief.

'Oh, here you are at last!' She clasped her hands above her head. And to me, she added, 'It wasn't until Andrzej was on his way to fetch you that I realized it's February the thirteenth today – unlucky thirteen!'

13 ~ Trouble and Strife Next Door

The artist's studio where I now found myself, and where I would have to stay for a while, was quite large, a spacious room with a glazed ceiling. It had windowless alcoves on both sides, closed off by doors. The Boguckis had got me a camp bed, and after the plank beds I had been sleeping on for so long it seemed wonderfully comfortable. I was very happy simply not seeing any Germans. Now I didn't have to listen to their yelling, or fear being beaten or even killed by an SS man at any moment. During these days I tried not to think of what still lay ahead of me before the war was over – if I lived until then. I was cheered by the news Mrs Bogucka brought one day: Soviet troops had retaken Kharkow. And yet, what was to become of me? I realized that I could not stay in the studio very long. Perkowski had to find a tenant in the next few days, if only because the Germans had announced a census which would entail a police search of all homes to see if the occupants were properly registered and had a right to live there. Potential tenants came to look at the room almost every day, and when they did I had to hide in one of the alcoves and lock its door on the inside.

After two weeks Bogucki came to an agreement with the former music director of Polish Radio, my pre-war boss Edmund Rudnicki, who arrived one evening with an engineer called Gębczyński. I was to move into the home of the engineer and his wife on the ground floor of the same building. That evening I touched a keyboard again for the first time in seven months. Seven months during which I had lost all my loved ones, survived the liquidation of the ghetto and helped to demolish its walls, heaving lime and stacks of bricks around. I resisted Mrs Gębczyńska's persuasions for some time, but finally gave in. My stiff fingers moved reluctantly over the keys and the sound was irritatingly strange, grating on my nerves.

The same evening I heard another piece of alarming news. Gębczyński had a phone call from a usually well-informed friend, who told him people were to be hunted down all over the city the next day. We were all extremely uneasy. However, it turned out to be a false alarm; there were many such at the time. Next day a former colleague from the radio station turned up, the conductor Czesław Lewicki, who later became a close friend of mine. He had a bachelor flat at number 83 Puławska Street at his disposal, but was not living there himself, and he had agreed to let me occupy it.

It was seven in the evening on Saturday, 27 February, when we left the Gębczyńskis' flat. Thank heavens it was pitch dark. We took a rickshaw in the Plac Unii, reached Puławska Street without mishap and raced up to the fourth floor, hoping not to meet anyone on the stairs.

The bachelor flat turned out to be comfortable and elegantly furnished. You went through a hall to get to the lavatory, and there was a large wall cupboard and a gas cooker on the other side of the hall. The room itself contained a comfortable divan, a wardrobe, a small bookshelf, a little table and some comfortable chairs. The small library was full of sheet music and scores, and there were some academic books as well. I felt I was in paradise. I did not sleep much that first night; I wanted to relish the comfort of lying on a real, well-sprung couch.

Next day Lewicki came with a friend, a doctor's wife called Mrs Malczewska, to bring my things. We discussed how I was to be fed and how I should manage about the census when it took place next day. I would have to spend all day in the lavatory, with the door locked on the inside, just as I had locked the alcove doors in the studio. Even if the Germans broke into the flat during the census, we concluded that they would be unlikely to notice the small door behind which I was hiding. At most, they would take it for the door of a locked cupboard.

I kept strictly to this strategic plan. Taking plenty of books, I went into the lavatory in the morning and waited patiently until evening – it was not exactly comfortable for a long period of time, and by that point I had dreamed of nothing since midday but being able to stretch my legs out. The entire manoeuvre proved superfluous; no one came except Lewicki, who looked in towards evening, both curious and anxious to find out how I was. He brought vodka, sausage, bread and butter with him, and we ate like kings. The idea of the census was to allow the Germans to track down all Jews hiding in Warsaw in one fell swoop. They had not found me, and I felt a new confidence.

Lewicki lived some way off, and he and I agreed that he would visit only twice a week, bringing food. I had to occupy the time between his eagerly awaited visits somehow or other. I read a great deal and learned to prepare delicious dishes, following the culinary advice of the doctor's wife. Everything had to be done without a sound. I moved about in slow motion, on tiptoe – God forbid I should knock a hand or foot against anything! The walls were thin, and any careless movement might give me away to my neighbours. I could hear what they were doing only too clearly, particularly the people next door on the left. Judging by their voices, the tenants of that flat were a young married couple who used to begin their conversation every evening with tender pet names for each other – 'Kitten' and 'Puppy-dog'. After about a quarter of an hour, however, domestic harmony would be disturbed, their voices rose, and the epithets they used were now drawn from the entire range of domesticated animals, ending with the pig. There was then what was presumably a reconciliation; the voices would be silent for some time, and then I would hear a third voice, the sound of a piano on which the young woman played with feeling – although she struck a number of wrong notes. However, her tinkling did not usually last long either. The music would stop, and an irritated female voice resumed the quarrel. 'Oh, very well, then, I'm not playing any more! You always turn away when I start playing.'

And they would begin running through the animal kingdom again.

As I listened, I often thought sadly how much I would give, and how happy I would be, if I could only get my hands on the tinny, out-of-tune old piano that caused such trouble and strife next door.

The days passed by. Either Mrs Malczewska or Lewicki visited me regularly twice a week, bringing food and news of the latest political developments. They were not encouraging: I was sorry to hear that the Soviet troops had withdrawn from Kharkow again, and the Allies were retreating from Africa. Doomed to inactivity, spending most days alone with my gloomy thoughts, brooding over and over again on my family's dreadful fate, I found my doubts and depression becoming worse. When I looked out of the window at the traffic, always the same, and saw the Germans moving about down there as calmly as ever, it seemed to me quite likely that this state of affairs might never end. And then what would become of me? After years of pointless suffering I would be discovered one day and killed. The best I could hope for was to commit suicide rather than fall into German hands alive.

My mood did not start to improve until the big Allied offensive in Africa began and was crowned by success after success. One hot day in May I was just making some soup for my midday meal when Lewicki appeared. Panting from running up to the fourth floor, he paused for breath just until he could gasp out the news he had brought: the German and Italian resistance in Africa had finally collapsed.

If only it had all started earlier! If the Allied troops had been winning victories in Europe rather than Africa at this point, perhaps I could have summoned up some enthusiasm. Perhaps the rising plotted and organized by the small remnant of Jews left in the Warsaw ghetto would have had at least a tiny chance of success then. Parallel to the increasingly good news that Lewicki brought were the increasingly dreadful details he had also heard of the tragic actions of my brothers: the handful of Jews who had decided to offer at least some active resistance to the Germans at this last, hopeless stage. From the underground papers I received I learned of the Jewish uprising, the battles for every building, for every section of every street, and the great losses suffered by the Germans. Even though artillery, tanks and the air force were called in during the battles in the ghetto it was weeks before they could suppress the rebels who were so

much weaker than themselves. No Jew was willing to be
taken alive. Once the Germans had captured a building the
women still inside it carried the children up to the top floor,
where they threw themselves and the children off the bal-
conies into the street below. If I leaned out of the window
in the evening, when it was time to sleep, I could see the
firelight to the north of Warsaw, and heavy masses of smoke
drifting over the clear, starry sky.

In early June Lewicki came to see me unexpectedly one
day, not at his accustomed time but at midday. This time he
was not the bearer of good news. He was unshaven, his eyes
were rimmed with dark circles as if he hadn't slept all night,
and his expression was visibly distressed.

'Get dressed!' he told me in a whisper.

'What's happened?'

'The Gestapo sealed my room at Dr and Mrs Malczewski's
yesterday evening. They could be here any moment. We
must get away at once.'

Get away? In broad daylight, at noon? It amounted to
suicide, at least as far as I was concerned. Lewicki was getting
impatient.

'Come on, come on!' he urged me, as I just stood there
instead of doing as he expected and packing a bag. He
decided to encourage and cheer me. 'Don't worry,' he began
nervously. 'Everything's been seen to. There's someone waiting for you not far off, ready to take you somewhere safe.'

I was still unwilling to move from the spot. What will be
will be, I thought. Lewicki would escape anyway and the
Gestapo would not find him. If the worst came to the worst,
I would rather put an end to my life here than risk wandering
the city again. I simply did not have the strength left for it.
Somehow I explained all this to my friend, and we embraced,

all but sure we would never meet again in this life. Then Lewicki left the flat.

I began pacing up and down the room that had seemed one of the safest places on earth, although now it felt like a cage. I was caught there like an animal, and it was only a matter of time before the slaughterers came to find and kill me. They would be delighted with their catch. I had never smoked before, but that day, as I waited for death, I smoked the whole pack of a hundred cigarettes Lewicki had left. But death delayed its coming hour by hour. I knew the Gestapo usually came in the evening or early in the morning. I did not undress, and put no lights on, but stared at the balcony rail visible through the window and listened for the slightest sound coming up from the street or the staircase. Lewicki's parting words still rang in my ears. His hand was already on the door-knob when he turned once more, came up to me, embraced me again and said, 'If they do come up and storm the flat, throw yourself off the balcony. You don't want them to get you alive!' And he added, to make it easier for me to decide on suicide, 'I have poison on me. They won't get me either.'

By now it was late. The traffic in the streets had died down entirely, and all the windows in the building opposite were darkened one by one. And still the Germans did not come. My nerves were stretched to breaking point. Sometimes I found myself wishing that if they had to come they would do so as soon as possible. I didn't want to suffer these torments any more. At some time that night I changed my mind about the manner of my suicide. It had suddenly occurred to me that I could hang myself instead of jumping off the balcony, and although I can't say why, this death seemed to me easier, a quiet way to go. Still without putting a light on,

I began searching the room for something to serve as a rope. Finally I found a long and quite stout piece of cord behind the books on the shelf.

I took down the picture hanging above the bookshelf, checked that the hook was firmly in the wall, made my noose ready – and waited. The Gestapo did not come.

They did not come in the morning either, and they stayed away for the next few days. But at eleven on Friday morning, as I was lying on the couch after an almost sleepless night, I heard shooting in the street. I hurried to the window. A line of police was strung out right across the entire width of the street, including the pavements, shooting chaotically and at random into the fleeing crowd. After a while some SS trucks drove up, and a large section of the street was surrounded – the section where my building stood. Groups of Gestapo officers went into all the buildings in that section and brought men out of them. They entered my building too.

There could be no doubt that they would find my hiding place now. I pushed a chair over to the bookshelf so that I could reach the picture hook more easily, prepared my noose and went to the door to listen. I could hear Germans shouting on the stairs a couple of floors lower down. Half an hour later all was still again. I looked out of the window. The blockade had been lifted, the SS trucks had driven away.

They had not come.

14 ~ Szałas' Betrayal

A week had passed since Lewicki's flight. Still the Gestapo did not come, and gradually my nerves calmed down. But there was another threat: my food supplies were running low. I had nothing left except a small quantity of beans and oatmeal. I limited my meals to two a day, and when I made soup I used only ten beans and a spoonful of oatmeal each time, but even portioned out in this way my provisions would not last beyond a few more days. One morning another Gestapo car drove up to the building where I was hiding. Two SS men carrying a piece of paper got out and entered the building. I was convinced they were looking for me, and I prepared for death. Yet again, however, I was not their quarry.

My provisions were all gone now. I had had nothing but water for two days. I had two alternatives: to die of starvation or risk going out to buy a loaf from the nearest street seller. I opted for the second. I shaved carefully, dressed, and left the building at eight in the morning, trying to walk in a casual way. No one took any notice of me, despite my obviously 'non-Aryan' features. I bought the loaf and went back to the flat. This was 18 July 1943. I lived on that single loaf – my money would not stretch to more – for ten whole days, until 28 July.

On 29 July, early in the afternoon, I heard a soft knocking at the door. I did not react. After a while a key was carefully put in the lock and turned, the door opened and a young man I did not know came in. He closed the door behind him quickly and asked, in a whisper, 'Nothing suspicious going on?'

'No.'

Only then did he turn his attention to me. He looked me up and down, amazement in his eyes. 'You're alive, then?'

I shrugged my shoulders. I supposed I looked sufficiently alive not to need to answer. The stranger smiled, and rather belatedly introduced himself: he was Lewicki's brother, and had come to tell me that food would be delivered next day. Some time in the next few days I would be taken elsewhere, for the Gestapo were still in search of Lewicki and might yet come here.

Sure enough, next day the engineer Gębczyński turned up with another man, whom he introduced to me as a radio technician called Szałas, a trustworthy underground activist. Gębczyński threw himself into my arms; he had been sure that I must have died of starvation and weakness by now. He told me all our mutual friends had been worried about me, but they could not approach the building, which was under constant observation by secret agents. As soon as the agents had moved off, he had been told to deal with my mortal remains and make sure I had a decent burial.

Szałas was to take care of me on a permanent basis from now on, a task assigned to him by our underground organization.

He proved a very dubious protector, however. He looked in every ten days with a tiny amount of food, explaining that he had been unable to scrape up the money for more. I gave him some of the few possessions I still had left to sell, but it nearly always transpired that they were stolen from him, and he turned up once again with a tiny quantity of food, only enough for two or three days, although it sometimes had to last two weeks. When I was finally lying on my bed, utterly exhausted by starvation and convinced I was about to die, Szałas would put in an appearance with a little food for me, just enough to keep me alive and give me the strength to continue tormenting myself. Beaming, evidently with his mind on something else, he would always enquire, 'Still alive, then, are you?'

I *was* still alive, even though the combination of malnutrition and grief had given me jaundice. Szałas did not take that too seriously, and told me the cheering tale of his grandfather, whose girlfriend jilted him when he suddenly went down with jaundice. Jaundice was nothing to speak of, in Szałas' opinion. By way of consolation, he told me that the Allies had landed in Sicily. Then he said goodbye and left. That was our last meeting, for he never turned up again, although ten days passed; and then the time stretched to twelve days, and then two weeks.

I was eating nothing, and had not even enough strength to get up and drag myself to the water tap. If the Gestapo had come now I would not have been able to hang myself. I dozed for most of the day, and when I woke it was only to suffer unbearable pangs of hunger. My face, arms and legs were already beginning to swell up when Mrs Malczewska came, unhoped for: I knew that she, her husband and Lewicki had been forced to leave Warsaw and go into hiding. She had firmly believed I was perfectly all right, and simply meant to look in for a chat and a cup of tea. I learned from her that Szałas had been collecting money for me all over Warsaw, and since no one would grudge it when a man's life was to be saved, he had amassed a handsome sum. He had assured my friends that he was visiting me almost daily and I wanted for nothing.

The doctor's wife left Warsaw again a few days later, but before she went she provided me with lavish food supplies, and promised me more reliable care. Unfortunately, it did not last long.

At midday on 12 August, just as I was making soup for myself as usual, I heard someone trying to break into the flat. This was not the way my friends knocked when they came to visit me; it was a hammering on the door. The Germans, then. However, after a while I identified the voices accompanying the banging as female. One woman shouted, 'Open this door at once, or we'll call the police!'

The hammering became more and more insistent. There could be no doubt about it; the other people in the building had found out that I was hidden there, and had decided to hand me in to avoid risking accusations of harbouring a Jew.

I hastily dressed and put my compositions and a few other things in a bag. The hammering stopped for a moment. No doubt the angry women, annoyed by my silence, were prepared to put their threat into action and were probably on their way to the nearest police station already. I quietly opened the door and slipped out into the stairway, only to come face to face with one of the women. She had obviously taken up her post there to make sure I did not escape. She barred my way.

'Are you from that flat in there?' She pointed at the door. 'You're not registered!'

I told her the tenant of the flat was a colleague of mine, and I'd just missed finding him at home. My explanation made no sense, and naturally it did not satisfy the bellicose woman.

'Let me see your pass, please! Your pass – at once!' she shouted even louder. Here and there other tenants of the building were putting their heads out of their doors, alarmed by the noise.

I pushed the woman aside and ran downstairs. I heard her screeching behind me. 'Shut the front door! Don't let him out!'

On the ground floor I rushed past the caretaker. Mercifully, she had failed to catch what the other woman was shouting down the stairs. I reached the entrance and ran out into the street.

I had escaped death yet again, but it still lay in wait for me. It was one o'clock in the afternoon, and here I stood in the street: unshaven, my hair uncut for many months, wearing a crumpled, shabby suit. Even without my Semitic features, I was bound to attract attention. I turned down a side street and hurried on. Where was I to go? The only acquaintances I had in the neighbourhood were the Boldoks, who lived in Narbutt Street. However, I was so nervous that I lost my way, although I knew the area well. For almost an hour I wandered through little streets until I finally reached my destination. I hesitated for a long time before I made up my mind to ring the bell in the hope of finding shelter behind that door, for I knew only too well how dangerous my presence would be to my friends. If I was found with them they would be shot too. Yet I had no alternative. No sooner had they opened the door than I instantly assured them I would not stay long; I just wanted to make some phone calls to see where I could find a new, permanent hiding place. But my phone calls were unsuccessful. Several of my friends could not take me in, others could not leave home because our organizations had successfully raided one of the biggest

Warsaw banks that day, and the whole city centre was surrounded by police. In view of this the Boldoks, an engineer
and his wife, decided to let me sleep in an empty flat on a
lower floor to which they had the keys. Next morning my
former radio colleague Zbigniew Jaworski arrived. He was
going to let me stay with him for a few days.

So I was safe for a while in the home of kind people who
wished me well! That first evening I took a bath, and then
we ate a delicious supper washed down with schnapps, which
unfortunately did my liver no good. None the less, despite
the pleasant atmosphere and, above all, the chance to talk
to my heart's content after months of enforced silence, I
planned to leave my hosts as soon as possible for fear of
endangering them, although Zofia Jaworska and her courageous mother Mrs Bobrownicka, an old lady of seventy,
urged me to stay with them as long as necessary.

All my attempts to find a new hiding place, meanwhile,
were frustrated. I came up against refusals on all sides.
People were afraid to take in a Jew; after all, the death
penalty was mandatory for the offence. I was feeling more
depressed than ever when providence came to my aid again
at the last moment, this time in the form of Helena Lewicka,
Mrs Jaworska's sister-in-law. We had not known each other
before, and this was the first time she had met me, but when
she heard of my previous experiences she instantly agreed
to take me in. She shed tears over my plight, although her
own life was not an easy one, and she herself had plenty
of reasons to mourn the fate of many of her friends and
relations.

On 21 August, after my last night with the Jaworskis, while
the Gestapo were roaming the neighbourhood and keeping
everyone on edge with worry and anxiety, I moved to a large

block of flats in Aleja Niepodległości. This was to be my last hiding place before the Polish rebellion and the complete destruction of Warsaw – a roomy fourth-floor bachelor flat entered direct from the stairway. It had electric light and gas, but no water; water was fetched from a communal tap on the landing, and the communal lavatory was there too. My neighbours were intellectuals, from a higher class than the tenants in Puławska Street. My immediate neighbours were a married couple active in the underground; they were on the run and did not sleep at home. This fact entailed some risk for me too, but I felt I would rather have such people as neighbours than semi-educated Poles loyal to their masters who might hand me over out of fear. The other buildings nearby were mainly occupied by Germans and housed various military authorities. A large unfinished hospital building with some kind of storeroom in it stood opposite my windows. Every day I saw Bolshevist prisoners of war hauling heavy crates in and out. This time I had ended up in one of the most German parts of Warsaw, right in the lion's den, which may in fact have made it a better, safer place for me.

I would have felt quite happy in my new hiding place if my health had not been going downhill so rapidly. My liver was giving me a great deal of trouble, and finally, in early December, I suffered such an attack of pain that it cost me a huge effort not to scream out loud. The attack lasted all night. The doctor called by Helena Lewicka diagnosed acute inflammation of the gall bladder and recommended a strict diet. Thank heaven I was not dependent on the 'care' of someone like Szałas this time; I was being looked after by Helena, the best and most self-sacrificing of women. With her help I gradually recovered my health.

And so I entered the year 1944.

I did all I could to lead as regular a life as possible. I studied English from nine to eleven in the morning, read from eleven to one, then made my midday meal, and returned to my English studies and my reading from three to seven.

Meanwhile the Germans were suffering defeat after defeat. Talk of counter-attacks had long since ceased. They were conducting a 'strategic withdrawal' from all fronts, an operation represented in the press as the surrender of unimportant areas so that the front line could be curtailed to German advantage. However, despite their defeats at the front the terror they spread within the countries they still occupied increased. Public executions in the streets of Warsaw had begun in the autumn and now took place almost every day. As ever, with their usual systematic approach to everything, they still had time to demolish the masonry of the ghetto, now 'cleansed' of its people. They destroyed building after building, street after street, and had the rubble taken out of the city by narrow-gauge railway. The 'masters of the world', whose honour had been injured by the Jewish uprising, were determined not to leave a stone standing.

At the beginning of the year an entirely unexpected event disturbed the monotony of my days. One day someone began trying to get in through my door – working on it at length, slowly and with determination, with pauses in between. At first I was not sure what this could mean. Only after much thought did I realize it was a burglar. This posed a problem. In the eyes of the law we were both criminals: I by the mere biological fact of being a Jew, he as a thief. So should I threaten him with the police once he got in? Or was it more likely that he would make the same threat to me? Should we hand each other over to the police, or make a non-aggression pact between criminals? In the end he did not break in; a tenant in the building had scared him away.

On 6 June 1944 Helena Lewicka visited me in the afternoon, beaming and bringing me the news that the Americans and the British had landed in Normandy; they had broken the German resistance and were advancing. Sensationally good news now came thick and fast: France was taken, Italy had surrendered, the Red army was on the Polish border, Lublin had been liberated.

Soviet air raids on Warsaw came more and more frequently; I could see the fireworks display from my window. There was a growling noise in the east, scarcely audible at first, then growing stronger and stronger: Soviet artillery. The Germans evacuated Warsaw, including the contents of the unfinished hospital building opposite. I watched with hope, and with a growing belief in my heart that I would live, and be free. On 29 July Lewicki came bursting in with the news that the rebellion in Warsaw would begin any day now. Our organizations were hastily buying weapons from the retreating, demoralized Germans. The purchase of a consignment of sub-machine guns had been entrusted to my never-to-be-forgotten host in Fałat Street, Zbigniew Jaworski. Unfortunately he met some Ukrainians, who were even worse than the Germans. On the pretext of handing over the weapons he had bought, they took him into the yard of the agricultural college and shot him there.

On 1 August Helena Lewicka came in just for a minute at four in the afternoon. She wanted to take me down to the cellar, because the rebellion was to begin in an hour's time. Guided by an instinct that had already saved me many times before, I decided to stay where I was. My protectress took leave of me, as if I were her son, with tears in her eyes. Her voice catching, she said, 'Shall we ever meet again, Władek?'

15 ~ In a Burning Building

Despite Helena Lewicka's assurances that the rebellion was to begin at five o'clock, in only a few minutes' time, I simply could not believe it. During the years of occupation political rumours had constantly circulated in the city, announcing events that never materialized. The evacuation of Warsaw by the Germans – something I had been able to observe from my window myself – the panic-stricken flight westward of overloaded trucks and private cars, had come to a halt in the last few days. And the thunder of the Soviet artillery, so close a few nights earlier, was now clearly moving away from the city and becoming weaker.

I went to the window: peace reigned in the streets. I saw the normal pedestrian traffic, perhaps rather less of it than usual, but this part of Aleja Niepodległości had never been very busy. A tram coming down the street from the technical university drew up at the stop. It was almost empty. A few people got out: women, an old man with a walking stick. And then three young men got out too, carrying long objects wrapped in newspaper. They stopped outside the first tram-car; one looked at his watch, then cast a glance around him, and suddenly he knelt down in the road, put the package he was carrying to his shoulder, and a series of rapid clattering sounds was heard. The newspaper at the end of packet began to glow, and revealed the barrel of a machine gun. At the same time the other two men nervously shouldered their own weapons.

The young man's shots were like a signal given to the neighbourhood: soon afterwards there was shooting everywhere, and when the explosions in the immediate vicinity died down you could hear shots coming from the city centre, any number of them. They followed close upon one another, never stopping, like the sound of water boiling in a huge kettle. It was as if the street had been swept clean. Only the elderly gentleman was still hurrying awkwardly along with the aid of his stick, obviously gasping for breath; it was difficult for him to run. Finally he too reached the entrance of a building and disappeared inside it.

I went to the door and put my ear against the wood. There was confused movement on the landing and in the stairway. Doors were flung open and slammed again, and people were running about in all directions. One woman cried, 'Jesus and Mary!' Another called in the direction of the stairs, 'Do be careful, Jerzy!' An answer came up from the lower floors. 'Yes, all right!' Now the women were weeping; one of them, obviously unable to control herself, was sobbing nervously. A deep bass voice tried calming her, in an undertone. 'It won't take long. After all, everyone's been waiting for this.'

This time Helena Lewicka's prediction had been correct: the rebellion had begun.

I lay down on the sofa to think what to do next.

When Mrs Lewicka had left she locked me in as usual, using the key to the flat and the padlock. I went back to the window. Groups of Germans were standing in the doorways of the buildings. Others came to join them from the direction of Pole Mokotowskie. They were all armed with semi-automatics, they wore helmets and had hand grenades in their belts. No fighting was going on in our part of the street. The Germans fired from time to time, but only at windows and people looking out of them. There was no return fire from the windows. Only when the Germans reached the corner of 6 August Street did they open fire both in the direction of the technical university and the opposite way, towards the 'filters' – the city waterworks. Perhaps I would be able to find my way to the city centre from the back of the building by making straight for the waterworks, but I had no weapon, and in any case I was locked in. If I began hammering on the door, would the neighbours take any notice, concerned as they were with their own affairs? And I would then have to ask them to go down to Helena Lewicka's friend, the only person in the building who knew I was hiding in this room. She held the keys so that if the worst came to the worst she could unlock the door and let me out. I decided to wait until morning and make up my mind what to do then, depending on what happened in the meantime.

By now there was a great deal more shooting. The rifle fire was interspersed with the louder explosions of hand grenades – or if artillery had been brought into action perhaps I was hearing shells. In the evening, as dark fell, I saw the first glow of the fires. The reflection of the flames, still infrequent, glowed here and there in the sky. They lit it up brightly, and then were extinguished. Gradually the shooting died down. There were only a few isolated explosions to be heard, and the brief rattle of machine-gun fire. The activity in the stairway of the building had died down too; the tenants had obviously barricaded themselves into their flats, so as to absorb their impressions of this first day of the rebellion in private. It was late when I suddenly fell asleep without undressing, and I slept the deep sleep of nervous exhaustion.

I woke equally suddenly in the morning. It was very early, and morning twilight had only just broken. The first sound I heard was the clatter of a horse-drawn cab. I went to the window. The cab passed by at an easy trot, its hood back, as if nothing had happened. Otherwise, the street was empty except for a man and a woman walking along the pavement under my windows with their hands in the air. From where I stood I could not see the Germans escorting them. Suddenly they both leaped forward and began to run. The woman cried out, 'Left, turn left!' The man was the first to turn aside, and disappeared from my field of vision. At that moment there was a volley of gunfire. The woman stopped, clutched her stomach and then fell gently to the ground like a sack, her legs folding under her. She did not really fall so much as sink to her knees, her right cheek coming to rest on the asphalt of the road, and she remained in this complicated acrobatic position. The brighter the daylight became, the more gunfire I heard. When the sun came up in the sky, a very clear sky in those days, the whole of Warsaw was echoing to rifle fire again, and the sound of heavy artillery began to mingle with it more and more frequently.

Around midday Mrs Lewicka's friend came upstairs with some food and news for me. So far as our quarter was concerned, the news was not good: it had been in German hands almost from the start, and there had only just been time for the young people of the resistance organizations to make their way through to the city centre as the rebellion began. Now there could be no question of even venturing out of the house. We would have to wait until detachments from the city centre relieved us.

'But I might be able to slip through somehow,' I protested.

She cast me a pitying look. 'Listen, you haven't been out

of doors for a year and a half! Your legs would give way before you were even halfway there.' She shook her head, held my hand and added soothingly, 'You'd better stay here. We'll see it through somehow.'

Despite everything her spirits were high. She took me to the window in the stairway, which gave a view from the side of the building opposite my own window. The whole residential complex of bungalows on the Staszic estate, right up to the waterworks, was in flames. You could hear the hissing of burning beams, the sound of ceilings falling in, people screaming, and shots. A reddish-brown pall of smoke covered the sky. When the wind briefly drove it aside, you could see the red and white flags on the distant horizon.

The days passed by. No help came from the city centre. For years now I had been used to hiding from everyone except a group of friends who knew that I was alive and where I was. I could not bring myself to leave the room, letting the other people in the block know I was here and having to enter into community life with them in our besieged flats. Knowing about me would only make them feel worse; if the Germans discovered, on top of everything else, that they were hiding a 'non-Aryan' in the building, they would be punished twice as severely. I decided to go on confining myself to eavesdropping through the door on the conversations in the stairway. The news did not improve: bitter battles were being fought in the city centre, no support was coming from outside Warsaw, and the German terror was growing in our part of the city. In Langiewicz Street, Ukrainians let the inhabitants of a building burn to death in its flames, and they shot the occupants of another block of flats. The famous actor Mariusz Mszyński was murdered quite close to this area.

The neighbour down below stopped visiting me. Perhaps some family tragedy had driven my existence out of her mind. My provisions were running out: they now consisted of nothing but a few rusks.

On 11 August the nervous tension in the building rose perceptibly. Listening at the door, I could not make out what was going on. All the tenants were on the lower floors, talking in raised voices which they then suddenly hushed. From the window I saw small groups of people slipping out of the surrounding buildings now and then and secretly making their way to ours. They left again later. Towards evening the tenants of the lower floors unexpectedly came running upstairs. Some of them were on my floor. I learned from their frightened whispering that there were Ukrainians in the building. On this occasion, however, they had not come to murder us. They were busy in the cellars for some time, took away the provisions stored down there and disappeared again. That evening I heard keys turn in the lock of my door and the padlock. Someone unlocked the door and removed the padlock, but did not come in; whoever it was ran quickly downstairs instead. What did that mean? The streets were full of leaflets that day. Someone had scattered them, but who?

On 12 August, about midday, panic broke out on the stairway again. Distracted people kept running up and down. I concluded, from scraps of conversation, that the building was surrounded by Germans and had to be evacuated at once because the artillery were about to destroy it. My first reaction was to get dressed, but next moment I realized that I could not go out into the street in view of the SS men unless I wanted to be shot on the spot. I heard firing from the street, and a sharp voice pitched unnaturally high calling,

'Everyone out, please! Leave your flats at once, please!'

I cast a glance at the stairway: it was quiet and empty. I climbed halfway down the stairs and went over to the window looking out on Sędziowska Street. A tank was pointing its gun at my floor of our building. Soon afterwards there was a spurt of fire, the gun jerked back, there was a roaring noise and a nearby wall fell over. Soldiers with their sleeves rolled up and tin cans in their hands were running about. Clouds of black smoke began rising up the outer wall of the building and through the stairway, from the ground floor up to my fourth floor. Some SS men ran into the building and hurried upstairs. I locked myself into the room, shook the contents of the small tube of strong sleeping tablets I had been taking while I had liver trouble out on my palm, and put my little bottle of opium ready to hand. I meant to swallow the tablets and drink the opium as soon as the Germans tried to open my door. But shortly afterwards, guided by an instinct that I could hardly have analysed rationally, I changed my plan: I left the room, hurried to the ladder leading from the landing to the attic, climbed up it, pushed the ladder away and closed the attic trapdoor after me. Meanwhile, the Germans were already hammering on the doors of the third-floor flats with the butts of their rifles. One of them came up to the fourth floor and entered my room. However, his companions presumably thought it dangerous to stay in the building any longer and began calling to him. 'Get a move on, Fischke!'

When the trampling down below moved away I crawled out of the attic, where I had almost been suffocated by the smoke coming up through the ventilation shafts from the flats below, and went back to my room. I indulged in the hope that only the ground-floor flats, set on fire as a deterrent, would burn, and the tenants would come back as soon as their papers had been checked. I picked up a book, made myself comfortable on the sofa, and began to read, but I could not take in a single word. I put the book down, closed my eyes, and decided to wait until I heard human voices somewhere near me.

I did not make up my mind to venture out on the landing again until dusk. My room was filling up with fumes and smoke now, and the red glow of firelight came in through the window from outside. The smoke on the stairway was so thick that you couldn't see the banisters. The loud, explosive crackle of the fire as it burnt more fiercely rose from the floors below, together with the crack of splitting wood and the crash of household items falling over. It would be impossible to use the stairs now. I went to the window. The building was surrounded by an SS cordon some distance away. There were no civilians in sight. Obviously the entire building was now burning, and the Germans were simply waiting for the fire to reach the upper floors and the roof timbers.

So this was to be my death in the end – the death I had been expecting for five years, the death I had escaped day after day until now it had finally caught up with me. I had often tried to imagine it. I expected to be captured and ill-treated, then shot or suffocated in the gas chamber. It had never occurred to me that I would burn alive.

I had to laugh at the ingenuity of fate. I was perfectly calm now, with a calm arising from my conviction that there was nothing more I could do to change the course of events. I let my glance wander round the room: its contours were indistinct as the smoke became thicker, and it looked strange and uncanny in the deepening twilight. I was finding it harder and harder to breathe. I felt dizzy, and there was a rushing sound in my head – the first effects of carbon-monoxide poisoning.

I lay down on the sofa again. Why let myself be burnt alive when I could avoid it by taking the sleeping tablets? How much easier my death would be than the deaths of my parents, sisters and brother, gassed in Treblinka! At these last moments I tried to think only of them.

I found the little tube of sleeping tablets, tipped the contents into my mouth and swallowed them. I was going to take the opium too, to make perfectly sure I died, but I had no time to do it. The tablets worked instantly on an empty, starved stomach.

I fell asleep.

16 ~ Death of a City

I did not die. Obviously the tablets had not been strong enough after all. I woke at seven in the morning, feeling nauseous. There was a roaring in my ears, the pulse at my temples was hammering painfully, my eyes were starting from their sockets and my arms and legs felt numb. It was a tickling sensation on my throat that had actually woken me. A fly was crawling over it, numbed as I was by the events of the night, and like me half dead. I had to concentrate and summon up all my strength to move my hand and swat it away.

My first emotion was not disappointment that I had failed to die, but joy to find myself alive. A boundless, animal lust for life at any price. I had survived a night in a burning building – now the main thing was to save myself somehow.

I lay where I was for a while to recover my senses a little more, then slipped off the sofa and crawled to the door. The room was still full of smoke, and when I reached for the door handle it was so hot that I let go of it again at once. At a second attempt, I mastered the pain and opened the door. There was less smoke on the stairway now than in my room, since it could easily find its way out through the charred openings of the tall landing windows. I could see the stairs; it would be possible to climb down them.

Summoning up all my willpower, I forced myself to stand

up, clutched the banisters, and began going downstairs. The floor below me was already burnt out and the fire had died down there. The door frames were still burning, and the air in the rooms beyond shimmered with heat. Remains of furniture and other possessions were still smouldering on the floors, leaving white heaps of ashes as the glow died out where they had stood.

As I came down to the first floor I found the burnt corpse of a man lying on the stairs; its clothes had carbonized on it, and it was brown and horribly bloated. I had to get past it somehow if I was to go on. I thought I would be able to raise my legs high enough to step over it as they dragged me forward. But at my first attempt my foot struck the stomach of the corpse and I stumbled, lost my balance, fell and rolled half a floor further down, together with the charred body. Fortunately the corpse was now behind me, and I could pick myself up and go on down to the ground floor. I came out into the yard, which was surrounded by a small wall covered with a creeper. I crawled over to this wall and hid in a niche in the corner, two metres from the burning building, camouflaging myself with the tendrils of the creeper and the leaves and stalks of some tomato plants growing between the wall and the building.

The shooting still did not let up. Bullets flew above my head, and I heard German voices close to me on the other side of the wall. They came from men walking down the pavement beside the road. Around evening cracks appeared in the wall of the burning building. If it collapsed I would be buried underneath it. However, I waited to move until it was dark, and until I had made more of a recovery from last night's poisoning. I went back to the stairway in the dark, but I dared not go up again. The interiors of the flats were still burning, just as they had been that morning, and the fire might reach my floor any moment. I thought hard, and devised a different plan: the huge, unfinished hospital building where the Wehrmacht kept its stores stood on the other side of Aleja Niepodległości. I would try to get there.

I went out into the street through the other entrance to my building. Although it was evening it was not completely dark. The broad roadway was lit up by the red glow of the fires. It was covered with corpses, and the woman I had seen killed on the second day of the rebellion still lay among them. I lay down on my stomach and began crawling towards the hospital. Germans were constantly passing by, alone or in groups, and when they did I stopped moving and pretended to be another corpse. The odour of decay rose from the dead bodies, mingling with the smell of the fires in the air. I tried to crawl as fast as I could, but the width of the road seemed endless and crossing it took for ever. At last I made it to the dark hospital building. I staggered through the first entrance I saw, collapsed on the floor and went to sleep at once.

Next morning I decided to explore the place. Much to my dismay, I found that the building was full of sofas, mattresses, pots and pans and china, items of everyday use, which meant the Germans would certainly be dropping in for them quite often. On the other hand, I found nothing to eat. I discovered a lumber room in a remote corner, full of old iron, pipes and stoves. I lay down and spent the next two days there.

On 15 August by my pocket calendar, which I kept with me, later on carefully crossing off day after day in it, I felt so unbearably hungry that I decided I must go and look for food of some kind whatever happened. In vain. I clambered up on the sill of a boarded-up window and began observing

the street through a small crack. Flies were swarming over
the bodies in the road. Not far away, on the corner of Filtrowa Street, stood a villa whose inhabitants had not yet
been thrown out of their home. They were leading an extraordinarily normal life, sitting on their terrace drinking tea.
A detachment of Wlassov soldiers commanded by the SS
moved up from 6 August Street. They collected the corpses
from the road, made a heap of them, poured petrol over it
and set it alight. At some point I heard steps coming my way
along the hospital passage. I got down from the window sill
and hid behind a crate. An SS man came into the room
where I was, looked round and went out again. I hurried out
into the passage, went to the staircase, ran up it and hid in
my lumber room. Soon afterwards a whole detachment
entered the hospital building to search all the rooms one by
one. They did not find my hiding place, although I heard
them laughing, humming to themselves and whistling, and I
also heard the vital question, 'Have we looked everywhere,
then?'

Two days later – and five days since I had last eaten anything – I set out in search of food and water once more.
There was no running water in the building, but buckets were
standing around in case of fire. The water they contained was
covered with an iridescent film and it was full of dead flies,
midges and spiders. I drank thirstily, all the same, but I had
to stop soon, for the water stank, and I could not avoid
swallowing dead insects. Then I found some crusts of bread
in the carpenter's workshop. They were mouldy, dusty and
covered with mouse droppings, but to me they were a treasure. Some toothless carpenter would never know he was
saving my life when he cut them off.

On 19 August the Germans threw the people in the villa

on the corner of Filtrowa Street out of their house, amidst much shouting and firing. I was now alone in this quarter of the city. The SS were visiting the building where I was hiding more and more often. How long could I survive in these conditions? A week? Two weeks? After that, suicide would be my only way of escape once again, and this time I had no means of committing suicide apart from a razor blade. I would have to cut my veins. I found a little barley in one of the rooms, and cooked it on the stove in the carpenter's workshop, which I heated by night, and that gave me something to eat for another few days.

On 30 August I decided to go back to the ruins of the building over the road, since it seemed to have finally burnt out now. I took a jug of water from the hospital with me and stole across the street at one in the morning. At first I thought of going down to the cellar, but the fuel there, coke and coal, was still smouldering because the Germans had kept setting fire to it again, so I hid in the ruins of a flat on the third floor. Its bathtub was full to the brim with water: dirty water, but still water. The fire had spared the larder, and I found a bag of rusks there.

After a week, visited by a terrible foreboding, I changed my hiding place again and moved up to the attic, or rather its bare boards, for the roof above them had fallen into the flames. That same day Ukrainians entered the building three times to search for loot in the undamaged parts of the flats. When they had gone I went down to the flat where I had been hiding for the last week. The fire had spared nothing but its tiled stove, and the Ukrainians had smashed that stove tile by tile, probably in search of gold.

Next morning the entire length of the Aleja Niepodległości was surrounded by soldiers. People carrying bundles on their backs, mothers with children clutching at them, were driven into this cordon. The SS and the Ukrainians brought many of the men out of the cordon and killed them in front of everyone for no reason at all, just as they did in the ghetto while it still stood. Had the rebellion ended in our defeat, then?

No: day by day heavy shelling tore the air again, making a sound like the flight of a horsefly – or to me, at close quarters, like the sound of old clocks being wound up – and then series of loud explosions could be heard coming rhythmically from the city centre.

Later, on 18 September, squadrons of aircraft flew over the city, parachuting supplies down to the rebels – whether of men or war material I don't know. Then aircraft bombed the parts of the city of Warsaw under German control and carried out airdrops over the city centre by night. The artillery fire from the east was getting stronger at the same time.

Not until 5 October did detachments of the rebels begin marching out of the city, surrounded by Wehrmacht men. Some were in uniform, some had only red and white armbands on their sleeves. They formed a curious contrast with the German detachments escorting them, who were in impeccable uniform, well-fed and self-confident, mocking and jeering at the failure of the rebellion as they filmed and photographed their new prisoners. The rebels, on the other hand, were thin, dirty, often ragged, and could keep on their feet only with difficulty. They paid no attention to the Germans, ignoring them entirely, as if they had chosen to march along the Aleja Niepodległości of their own free will. They kept discipline in their own ranks, supporting those who had difficulty in walking, and they did not so much as glance at the ruins, but marched on looking straight ahead. Although they were such a wretched sight beside their conquerors, you felt it was not they who were defeated.

After that, the exodus of the remaining civilian population from the city in ever smaller groups took another eight days. It was like seeing the life-blood flow from the body of a murdered man, first vigorously and then more slowly. The last people left on 14 October. Twilight had long fallen when a little company of laggards, their SS escorts urging them to make haste, passed the building where I was still hiding. I leaned out of the window, which was burnt out by the fire, and watched the hurrying figures bowed under the weight of their bundles until the darkness had swallowed them up.

Now I was alone, with a tiny quantity of rusks at the bottom of the bag and several bathtubs of dirty water as my entire stock of provisions. How much longer could I hold out in these circumstances, in view of the coming autumn with its shorter days and the threat of approaching winter?

17 ~ Life for Liquor

I was alone: alone not just in a single building or even a single part of a city, but alone in a whole city that only two months ago had had a population of a million and a half and was one of the richer cities of Europe. It now consisted of the chimneys of burnt-out buildings pointing to the sky, and whatever walls the bombing had spared: a city of rubble and ashes under which the centuries-old culture of my people and the bodies of hundreds of thousands of murdered victims lay buried, rotting in the warmth of these late autumn days and filling the air with a dreadful stench.

People visited the ruins only by day, riff-raff from outside the city furtively slinking about with shovels over their shoulders, scattering through the cellars in search of loot. One of them chose my own ruined home. He mustn't find me here; no one was to know of my presence. When he came up the stairs and was only two floors below me, I roared in a savage, threatening voice, 'What's going on? Get out! *Rrraus!*'

He shot away like a startled rat: the last of the wretched, a man scared off by the voice of the last poor devil left alive here.

Towards the end of October I was looking down from my attic and saw the Germans picking up one of these packs of hyenas. The thieves tried to talk their way out of trouble. I heard them repeating again and again, 'From Pruszków, from Pruszków,' and pointing to the west. The soldiers stood four of the men up against the nearest wall and shot them with their revolvers, despite their whimpering pleas for their lives. They ordered the rest to dig a grave in the garden of one of the villas, bury the bodies and get out. After that even the thieves kept away from this part of the city. I was the only living soul here now.

The first day of November was approaching, and it was beginning to get cold, particularly at night. To keep myself from going mad in my isolation, I decided to lead as disciplined a life as possible. I still had my watch, the pre-war Omega I treasured as the apple of my eye, along with my fountain pen. They were my sole personal possessions. I conscientiously kept the watch wound and drew up a timetable by it. I lay motionless all day long to conserve what little strength I had left, putting out my hand only once, around midday, to fortify myself with a rusk and a mug of water sparingly portioned out. From early in the morning until I took this meal, as I lay there with my eyes closed, I went over in my mind all the compositions I had ever played, bar by bar. Later, this mental refresher course turned out to have been useful: when I went back to work I still knew my repertory and had almost all of it in my head, as if I had been practising all through the war. Then, from my midday meal until dusk, I systematically ran through the contents of all the books I had read, mentally repeating my English vocabulary. I gave myself English lessons, asking myself questions and trying to answer them correctly and at length.

When darkness came I fell asleep. I would wake around one in the morning and go in search of food by the light of matches – I had found a supply of them in the building, in a flat that had not been entirely burnt out. I looked in cellars and the charred ruins of the flats, finding a little oatmeal here, a few pieces of bread there, some dank flour, water in tubs, buckets and jugs. I don't know how many times I passed the charred body on the stairs during these expeditions. He was the sole companion whose presence I need not fear. Once I found an unexpected treasure in a cellar: half a litre of spirits. I decided to save it until the end of the war came.

By day, as I lay on the floor, Germans or Ukrainians would often come into the building in search of loot. Each of these visitations was another strain on my nerves, for I was mortally afraid they would find me and murder me. Yet somehow or other they always left the attic alone, although I counted more than thirty such flying visits.

The fifteenth of November came, and the first snow fell. The cold weather troubled me more and more under the pile of rags I had collected to keep myself warm. Now they were thickly covered with soft white snow when I woke in the morning. I had made my bed in a corner under a part of the roof that was still intact, but the rest of it was gone, and large quantities of snow blew in from all sides. One day I stretched a piece of fabric under a broken window pane I had found and examined myself in this improvised mirror. At first I could not believe that the dreadful sight I saw was really myself: my hair had not been cut for months, and I was unshaven and unwashed. The hair on my head was thickly matted, my face was almost covered with a growth of dark beard, quite heavy by now, and where the beard did not cover it my skin was almost black. My eyelids were reddened, and I had a crusted rash on my forehead.

But what tormented me most was not knowing what was happening in the battle areas, both on the front and among the rebels. The Warsaw rebellion itself had been put down.

I could cherish no illusions about that. But perhaps there was' still resistance outside the city, in Praga on the other side of the Vistula. I could still hear artillery fire over there now and then, and shells would explode in the ruins, often quite near me, echoing harshly in the silence amidst the burnt-out buildings. What about resistance in the rest of Poland? Where were the Soviet troops? What progress was the Allied offensive making in the west? My life or death depended on the answer to these questions, and even if the Germans did not discover my hiding place it was soon going be my death – of cold if not starvation.

After seeing my reflection I decided to use some of my sparse water supply to have a wash, and at the same time I would light a fire in one of the few intact kitchen stoves to cook the remains of my oatmeal. I had eaten nothing warm for almost four months, and as the cold autumn weather came on I was suffering more and more from the lack of hot food. If I was to wash myself and cook something, I had to leave my hiding place by day. It was not until I was already on the stairs that I noticed a troop of Germans outside the military hospital opposite, working on its wooden fence. However, I had so set my heart on some hot porridge that I did not turn back. I felt I would fall ill if I did not warm my stomach with that porridge here and now.

I was already busy at the stove when I heard SS men striding up the stairs. I left the flat as fast as I could and hurried up to the attic. I made it! Once again, the Germans simply sniffed around and then went away. I went back down to the kitchen. In order to light a fire I had to shave chips off a door with a rusty knife I had found, and in doing so I got a splinter a centimetre long under my right thumbnail. It was so deeply and firmly embedded that I could not pull it out. This tiny accident could have dangerous consequences: I had no disinfectant, I was living in filthy surroundings, and I could easily get blood poisoning. Even if I looked on the bright side and assumed the blood poisoning would be confined to my thumb, it could well be left deformed, and my career as a pianist would be at risk, always supposing I survived until the end of the war.

I decided to wait until next day and then, if necessary, cut through the nail with my razor blade.

I was standing there looking ruefully at my thumb when I heard footsteps again. I swiftly set off for the attic once more, but this time it was too late. I found myself facing a soldier in a steel helmet carrying a rifle. His face was blank and not very intelligent.

He was as alarmed as I was by this lonely encounter in the ruins, but he tried to seem threatening. He asked, in broken Polish, what I was doing here. I said I was living outside Warsaw now and had come back to fetch some of my things. In view of my appearance, this was a ridiculous explanation. The German pointed his gun at me and told me to follow him. I said I would, but my death would be on his conscience, and if he let me stay here I would give him half a litre of spirits. He expressed himself agreeable to this form of ransom, but made it very clear that he would be back, and then I would have to give him more strong liquor. As soon as I was alone I climbed quickly to the attic, pulled up the ladder and closed the trapdoor. Sure enough, he was back after quarter of an hour, but accompanied by several other soldiers and an NCO. At the sound of their footsteps and voices I clambered up from the attic floor to the top of the intact piece of roof, which had a steep slope. I lay flat on my stomach with my feet braced against the gutter. If it had buckled or given way, I would have slipped to the roofing sheet and then fallen five floors to the street below. But the gutter held, and this new and indeed desperate idea for a hiding place meant that my life was saved once again. The Germans searched the whole building, piling up tables and chairs, and finally came up to my attic, but it did not occur to them to look on the roof. It must have seemed impossible for anyone to be lying there. They left empty-handed, cursing and calling me a number of names.

I was profoundly shaken by this encounter with the Germans, and decided that from now on I would lie on the roof by day, and climb down to the attic only when night came. The metal chilled me, my arms and legs were stiff and my body numb from my uncomfortable, tense position, but I had already endured so much that it was worth suffering a little more, although it was a week before the troop of Germans who knew I was hiding here finished their work on the hospital and left this part of the city again.

Today the SS were driving a group of men in civilian clothing to work on the hospital. It was nearly ten in the morning, and I was lying flat on the steep roof when I suddenly heard a volley of firing quite close to me, from a rifle or machine pistol: it was a sound between whistling and twittering, as if a flock of sparrows were flying overhead, and shots fell around me. I looked round: two Germans were standing on the hospital roof opposite, firing at me. I slid back down into the attic and ran to the trapdoor, ducking. Shouts of, 'Stop, stop!' pursued me as bullets flew overhead. However, I landed in the stairway safely.

There was no time to stop and think: my last hiding place in this building had been discovered, and I must leave it at once. I raced down the stairs and out into Sędziowska Street,

ran along the road and plunged into the ruins of the bungalows that had once been the Staszic estate.

Yet again my situation was hopeless, as it had been so
often before. I was wandering among the walls of totally
burnt-out buildings where there could not possibly be any
water or remnants of food, or even a hiding place. After a
while, however, I saw a tall building in the distance, facing
Aleja Niepodległości and backing on to Sędziowska Street,
the only multi-storey building in the area. I set off. On closer
inspection I saw that the centre of the building had been
burnt out, but the wings were almost intact. There was furniture in the flats, the tubs were still full of water from the
time of the rebellion, and the looters had left some provisions
in the larders.

Following my usual custom, I moved into the attic. The
roof was quite intact, with just a few holes left in it by splin-
ters of shrapnel. It was much warmer here than in my
previous hiding place, although flight from it would be
impossible. I could not even escape into death by jumping
off the roof. There was a small stained-glass window on the
last mezzanine floor of the building, and I could observe the
neighbourhood through it. Comfortable as my new surroundings were, I did not feel at ease here – perhaps just because
I was now used to the other building. All the same, I had
no choice: I must stay here.

I went down to the mezzanine floor and looked out of the
window. Below me were hundreds of burnt-out villas, an
entire part of the city now dead. The mounds of countless
graves stood in the little gardens. A troop of civilian workers
with spades and picks over their shoulders was going down
Sędziowska Street, marching four abreast. There was not a
single uniformed German with them. Still nervous and agi-

tated by my recent flight, I was seized by a sudden longing
to hear human speech, and my own voice replying. Come
what may, I would exchange a few words with these men. I
ran quickly downstairs and out into the street. By now the
working party was some way further on. I ran and caught
up with them.

'Are you Poles?'

They stopped, and looked at me in surprise. The leader
of the party replied, 'Yes.'

'What are you doing here?' Talking seemed difficult after
four months of absolute silence, apart from the couple of
remarks I had exchanged with the soldier from whom I ran-
somed myself with the liquor, and I felt deeply moved.

'Digging fortifications. What are you doing here yourself?'

'Hiding.'

The leader looked at me, I thought, with a touch of pity.
'Come with us,' he said. 'You can work, and you'll get some
soup.'

Soup! The mere idea of the chance of a bowl of real hot
soup made my stomach cramp with hunger so badly that for
a moment I was prepared to go with them, even if I was
killed later. I wanted that soup; I just wanted enough to eat
for once! But common sense prevailed.

'No,' I said. 'I'm not going to the Germans.'

The leader grinned, half cynical, half mocking. 'Oh, I don't
know,' he protested. 'The Germans aren't so bad.'

Only now did I realize what I had somehow failed to notice
before: the leader was the only one who spoke to me, while
all the others remained silent. He was wearing a coloured
armband on his sleeve, stamped with a mark. There was an
unpleasant, shifty, abject expression on his face. He did not

look me in the eye as he spoke but past me, over my right shoulder.

'No,' I repeated. 'Thanks, but no.'

'Just as you like,' he growled.

I turned to go. As the troop moved off again, I called, 'Goodbye!' after them.

Full of foreboding, or perhaps guided by an instinct for self-preservation that had been well honed over my years in hiding, I did not return to the attic of the building where I had decided to stay. I made for the nearest villa, as if the cellar there was my hiding place. When I reached its charred doorway I looked round again: the troop was going on its way, but the leader kept looking back to see where I went.

Not until they were out of sight did I return to my attic, or rather to the top mezzanine floor to look out of the window. Within ten minutes the civilian with the armband was back with two policemen. He pointed out the villa into which he had seen me go. They searched it, and then some of the neighbouring houses, but they never entered my building. Perhaps they were afraid of coming upon a large group of rebels still lurking in Warsaw. A number of people escaped with their lives during the war because of the cowardice of the Germans, who liked to show courage only when they felt they greatly outnumbered their enemies.

After two days I went in search of food. This time I planned to lay in a good supply so that I did not have to leave my hiding place too often. I would have to search by day, since I did not know this building well enough to find my way around it by night. I found a kitchen, and then a larder containing several cans of food and some bags and boxes. Their contents would have to be carefully checked. I untied strings and lifted lids. I was so absorbed in my search that I never heard anything until a voice right behind me said, 'What on earth are you doing here?'

A tall, elegant German officer was leaning against the kitchen dresser, his arms crossed over his chest.

'What are you doing here?' he repeated. 'Don't you know the staff of the Warsaw fortress commando unit is moving into this building any time now?'

18 ~ Nocturne in C sharp minor

I slumped on the chair by the larder door. With the certainty of a sleepwalker, I suddenly felt that my strength would fail me if I tried to escape this new trap. I sat there groaning and gazing dully at the officer. It was some time before I stammered, with difficulty, 'Do what you like to me. I'm not moving from here.'

'I've no intention of doing anything to you!' The officer shrugged his shoulders. 'What do you do for a living?'

'I'm a pianist.'

He looked at me more closely, and with obvious suspicion. Then his glance fell on the door leading from the kitchen to the other rooms. An idea seemed to have struck him.

'Come with me, will you?'

We went into the next room, which had obviously been the dining room, and then into the room beyond it, where a piano stood by the wall. The officer pointed to the instrument.

'Play something!'

Hadn't it occurred to him that the sound of the piano would instantly attract all the SS men in the vicinity? I looked enquiringly at him and did not move. He obviously sensed my fears, since he added reassuringly, 'It's all right, you can play. If anyone comes, you hide in the larder and I'll say it was me trying the instrument out.'

When I placed my fingers on the keyboard they shook. So

this time, for a change, I had to buy my life by playing the piano! I hadn't practised for two and a half years, my fingers were stiff and covered with a thick layer of dirt, and I had not cut my nails since the fire in the building where I was hiding. Moreover, the piano was in a room without any window panes, so its action was swollen by the damp and resisted the pressure of the keys.

I played Chopin's Nocturne in C sharp minor. The glassy, tinkling sound of the untuned strings rang through the empty flat and the stairway, floated through the ruins of the villa on the other side of the street and returned as a muted, melancholy echo. When I had finished, the silence seemed even gloomier and more eerie than before. A cat mewed in a street somewhere. I heard a shot down below outside the building – a harsh, loud German noise.

The officer looked at me in silence. After a while he sighed, and muttered, 'All the same, you shouldn't stay here. I'll take you out of the city, to a village. You'll be safer there.'

I shook my head. 'I can't leave this place,' I said firmly.

Only now did he seem to understand my real reason for hiding among the ruins. He started nervously.

'You're Jewish?' he asked.

'Yes.'

He had been standing with his arms crossed over his chest; he now unfolded them and sat down in the armchair by the piano, as if this discovery called for lengthy reflection.

'Yes, well,' he murmured, 'in that case I see you really can't leave.'

He appeared to be deep in thought again for some time, and then turned to me with another question. 'Where are you hiding?'

'In the attic.'

'Show me what it's like up there.'

We went upstairs. He inspected the attic with a careful and expert eye. In so doing he discovered something I had not yet noticed: a kind of extra floor above it, a loft made of boards under the roof valley and directly above the entrance to the attic itself. At first glance you hardly noticed it because the light was so dim there. The officer said he thought I should hide in this loft, and he helped me look for a ladder in the flats below. Once I was up in the loft I must pull the ladder up after me.

When we had discussed this plan and put it into action, he asked if I had anything to eat.

'No,' I said. After all, he had taken me unawares while I was searching for supplies.

'Well, never mind,' he added hastily, as if ashamed in retrospect of his surprise attack. 'I'll bring you some food.'

Only now did I venture a question of my own. I simply could not restrain myself any longer. 'Are you German?'

He flushed, and almost shouted his answer in agitation, as if my question had been an insult. 'Yes, I am! And ashamed of it, after everything that's been happening.'

Abruptly, he shook hands with me and left.

Three days passed before he reappeared. It was evening, and pitch dark, when I heard a whisper under my loft. 'Hello, are you there?'

'Yes, I'm here,' I replied.

Soon afterwards something heavy landed beside me. Through the paper, I felt several loaves and something soft, which later turned out to be jam wrapped in greaseproof paper. I quickly put the package to one side and called, 'Wait a moment!'

The voice in the dark sounded impatient. 'What is it? Hurry up. The guards saw me come in here, and I mustn't stay long.'

'Where are the Soviet troops?'

'They're already in Warsaw, in Praga on the other side of the Vistula. Just hang on a few more weeks – the war will be over by spring at the latest.'

The voice fell silent. I did not know if the officer was still there, or if he had gone. But suddenly he spoke again, 'You must hang on, do you hear?' His voice sounded harsh, almost as if he were giving an order, convincing me of his unyielding belief that the war would end well for us. Only then did I hear the quiet sound of the attic door closing.

Monotonous, hopeless weeks passed by. I heard less and less artillery fire from the direction of the Vistula. There were days when not a single shot broke the silence. I don't know whether I might not finally have given way at this time and committed suicide, as I had planned so many times before, if it hadn't been for the newspapers in which the German wrapped the bread he brought me. They were the latest, and I read them again and again, fortifying myself with the news they contained of German defeats on all the fronts. Those fronts were advancing with increasing speed further and further into the Reich.

The staff of the unit continued its work as before in the side wings of the building. Soldiers went up and down the stairs, often bringing large packages up to the attic and fetching others down, but my hiding place was well chosen; no one ever thought of searching the loft. There were guards constantly marching back and forth along the road outside the building. I heard their footsteps all the time, day and night, and their stamping as they warmed up their cold feet.

When I needed water I slipped by night into the wrecked
flats, where the bathtubs were full to the brim.

On 12 December the officer came for the last time. He
brought me a larger supply of bread than before and a warm
eiderdown. He told me he was leaving Warsaw with his
detachment, and I must on no account lose heart, since the
Soviet offensive was expected any day now.

'In Warsaw?'

'Yes.'

'But how will I survive the street fighting?' I asked
anxiously.

'If you and I have survived this inferno for over five years,'
he replied, 'it's obviously God's will for us to live. Well, we
have to believe that, anyway.'

We had already said goodbye, and he was about to go,
when an idea came to me at the last moment. I had long
been racking my brains for some way of showing him my
gratitude, and he had absolutely refused to take my only
treasure, my watch.

'Listen!' I took his hand and began speaking urgently. 'I
never told you my name – you didn't ask me, but I want you
to remember it. Who knows what may happen? You have a
long way to go home. If I survive, I'll certainly be working
for Polish Radio again. I was there before the war. If anything
happens to you, if I can help you then in any way, remember
my name: Szpilman, Polish Radio.'

He smiled his usual smile, half deprecating, half shy and
embarrassed, but I felt I had given him pleasure with what,
in the present situation, was my naïve wish to help him.

The first hard frosts came in the middle of December.
When I went out looking for water on the night of 13
December, I found it frozen everywhere. I fetched a kettle

and a pan from a flat near the back entrance of the building that the fire had spared, and returned to my loft. I shaved some ice from the contents of the pan and put it in my mouth, but it did not quench my thirst. I thought of another idea: I got under my eiderdown and put the pan of ice on my naked stomach. After a while the ice began to thaw, and I had water. I did the same over the next few days, for the temperature remained freezing.

Christmas came, and then the New Year, 1945: the sixth Christmas and New Year celebrations of the war, and the worst I had known. I was not in any condition to celebrate. I lay in the dark, listening to the stormy wind tearing at the roof sheeting and the damaged gutters that dangled down the walls of buildings, blowing down the furniture in those flats that were not entirely destroyed. In the intervals between the gusts that kept howling around the ruins I heard the squeaking and rustling of mice or even rats running back and forth in the attic. Sometimes they scurried over my eiderdown, and when I was asleep they ran over my face, scratching me with their claws as they passed swiftly by. In my mind, I went over every Christmas before and during the war. At first I had a home, parents, two sisters and a brother. Then we had no home of our own any more, but we were together. Later I was alone, but surrounded by other people. And now I was lonelier, I supposed, than anyone else in the world. Even Defoe's creation, Robinson Crusoe, the prototype of the ideal solitary, could hope to meet another human being. Crusoe cheered himself by thinking that such a thing could happen any day, and it kept him going. But if any of the people now around me came near I would need to run for it and hide in mortal terror. I had to be alone, entirely alone, if I wanted to live.

On 14 January unusual noises in the building and the street outside woke me. Cars drove up and then away again, soldiers ran up and down the stairs, and I heard agitated, nervous voices. Items were being carried out of the building all the time, probably to be loaded into vehicles. Early in the morning of 15 January, the sound of artillery from the previously silent front on the Vistula was heard. The shells did not reach the part of the city where I was hiding. However, the ground and the walls of the building shook under the constant dull thunder, the metal sheeting on the roof vibrated and plaster flaked from the interior walls. The sound must come from the famous Soviet Katyusha rockets of which we had heard so much even before the rebellion. In my delight and excitement I committed what, in my present circumstances, was an inexcusable piece of folly: I drank a whole pan of water.

Three hours later the heavy artillery fire died down again, but I was as nervous as ever. I did not sleep at all that night: if the Germans were going to defend the ruins of Warsaw, the street fighting would begin at any moment and I could be killed as the finale to all my earlier tribulations.

But the night passed peacefully. Around one o'clock I heard the remaining Germans leaving the building. Silence fell, a silence such as even Warsaw, a dead city for the last three months, had not known before. I could not even hear the steps of the guards outside the building. I didn't understand it. Was there any fighting going on?

Not until the early hours of the next day was the silence broken by a loud and resonant noise, the last sound I had expected. Radio loudspeakers set up somewhere nearby were broadcasting announcements in Polish of the defeat of Germany and the liberation of Warsaw.

The Germans had withdrawn without a fight.

As soon as it began to get light I prepared feverishly for my first venture out. My officer had left me a German military overcoat to keep me from freezing as I went in search of water, and I had already put it on when I suddenly heard the rhythmic footsteps of guards out in the road again. Had the Soviet and Polish troops withdrawn, then? I sank on my mattress, utterly dejected, and lay there until something new came to my ears: the voices of women and children, sounds I had not heard for months, women and children talking calmly just as if nothing had happened. It was like the old days, when mothers could simply walk down the street with their young ones. At all costs, I had to get information. This uncertainty was becoming unbearable. I ran downstairs, put my head out of the front door of the abandoned building, and looked out into Aleja Niepodległości. It was a grey, misty morning. To my left, not far away, stood a woman soldier in a uniform that was difficult to identify at this distance. A woman with a bundle on her back was approaching from my right. When she came closer I ventured to speak to her:

'Hello. Excuse me . . .' I called in a muted voice, beckoning her over.

She stared at me, dropped her bundle and took to her heels with a shriek of, 'A German!' Immediately the guard turned, saw me, aimed and fired her machine pistol. The bullets hit the wall and sent plaster flaking down on me. Without thinking, I rushed up the stairs and took refuge in the attic.

Looking out of my little window a few minutes later, I saw that the whole building was already surrounded. I heard soldiers calling to each other as they went down into the cellars, and then the sound of shots and exploding hand grenades.

This time my situation was absurd. I was going to be shot by Polish soldiers in liberated Warsaw, on the very verge of freedom, as the result of a misunderstanding. Feverishly, I began to wonder how I could make them realize, very quickly, that I was Polish before they dispatched me to the next world as a German in hiding. Meanwhile, another detachment wearing blue uniforms had arrived outside the building. I learned later that they were a detachment of railway police who happened to be passing and had been recruited to help the soldiers. So now I had two armed units after me.

I began slowly coming down the stairs, shouting as loud as I could, 'Don't shoot! I'm Polish!'

Very soon I heard swift footsteps climbing the stairs. The figure of a young officer in Polish uniform, with the eagle on his cap, came into view beyond the banisters. He pointed a pistol at me and shouted, 'Hands up!'

I repeated my cry of, 'Don't shoot! I'm Polish!'

The lieutenant went red with fury. 'Then why in God's name don't you come down?' he roared. 'And what are you doing in a German coat?'

Only when the soldiers had taken a closer look at me and reviewed the situation did they really believe I wasn't German. Then they decided to take me back to their headquarters so that I could wash and have a meal, although I was not yet sure what else they meant to do with me.

However, I could not go with them just like that. First, I had to keep a promise I had made myself that I would kiss the first Pole I met after the end of Nazi rule. Fulfilling my vow proved far from easy. The lieutenant resisted my suggestion for a long time, defending himself with all kinds of arguments except the one he was too kind-hearted to put forward. Not until I had finally kissed him did he produce a small mirror and hold it up to my face, saying with a smile, 'There, now you can see what a good patriot I am!'

After two weeks, well cared for by the military, clean and rested, I walked through the streets of Warsaw without fear, a free man, for the first time in almost six years. I was going east towards the Vistula to Praga – it used to be a remote, poor suburb, but it was now all there was of Warsaw, since the Germans had not destroyed what was left of it.

I was walking down a broad main road, once busy and full of traffic, its whole length now deserted. There was not a single intact building as far as the eye could see. I kept having to walk round mountains of rubble, and was sometimes obliged to climb over them as if they were scree slopes. My feet became entangled in a confused mess of ripped telephone wires and tramlines, and scraps of fabric that had once decorated flats or clothed human beings now long since dead.

A human skeleton lay by the wall of a building, under a rebel barricade. It was not large, and the bone structure was delicate. It must be the skeleton of a girl, since long blond hair could still be seen on the skull. Hair resists decay longer than any other part of the body. Beside the skeleton lay a rusty carbine, and there were remnants of clothing around the bones of the right arm, with a red and white armband where the letters AK had been shot away.

There are not even such remains left of my sisters, beautiful Regina and youthful, serious Halina, and I shall never find a grave where I could go to pray for their souls.

I stopped for a little rest, to draw breath. I looked over to the north of the city, where the ghetto had been, where half a million Jews had been murdered – there was nothing left of it. The Germans had flattened even the walls of the burnt-out buildings.

Tomorrow I must begin a new life. How could I do it, with nothing but death behind me? What vital energy could I draw from death?

I went on my way. A stormy wind rattled the scrap-iron in the ruins, whistling and howling through the charred cavities of the windows. Twilight came on. Snow fell from the darkening, leaden sky.

Postscript

About two weeks later one of my Polish Radio colleagues, the violinist Zygmunt Lednicki, who had taken part in the rebellion, came back to Warsaw after his wanderings. Like many others he had come on foot, wishing to be back in his own city as soon as possible. He had passed a temporary camp for German prisoners of war on the way. When he told me about it later my colleague added immediately that he did not approve of his own behaviour, but he had simply been unable to restrain himself. He went up to the tangle of barbed wire and said to the Germans, 'You always claimed to be a cultured people, but you took everything I had from me, a musician – my violin!' Then an officer rose with difficulty from the place where he was lying and staggered over to the wire. He looked wretched and shabby, with stubble on his face. Fixing despairing eyes on Lednicki, he asked, 'Do you happen to know a Mr Szpilman?'

'Yes, of course I do.'

'I'm a German,' the man whispered feverishly, 'and I helped Szpilman when he was hiding in the attic of the fortress commando unit in Warsaw. Tell him I'm here. Ask him to get me out. I beg you—'

At that moment one of the guards came up. 'You're not allowed to talk to the prisoners. Please go away.'

Lednicki went away. But next moment it struck him that he did not know the German's name. So he turned back, but the guard had now led the officer away from the fence.

'What's your name?' he called.

The German turned and shouted something, but Lednicki could not make it out.

And I did not know the officer's name myself. I had intentionally preferred to remain in ignorance of it, so that if I were captured and interrogated, and the German police asked who had been supplying me with bread from the army stores, I could not give his name away under torture.

I did everything in my power to track down the German prisoner, but I never managed to find him. The POW camp had been moved, and its whereabouts was a military secret. But perhaps that German – the *one human being* wearing German uniform that I met – perhaps he got safely home again.

I sometimes give recitals in the building at number 8 Narbutt Street in Warsaw where I carried bricks and lime – where the Jewish brigade worked: the men who were shot once the flats for German officers were finished. The officers did not enjoy their fine new homes for long. The building still stands, and there is a school in it now. I play to Polish children who do not know how much human suffering and mortal fear once passed through their sunny schoolrooms.

I pray they may never learn what such fear and suffering are.

Extracts from the Diary of Captain Wilm Hosenfeld

18 January 1942

The National Socialist revolution seems half-hearted in every way. History tells us of dreadful deeds and appalling barbarities during the French Revolution. And the Bolshevik Revolution too allowed terrible atrocities to be perpetrated on the ruling class by the animal instincts of subhuman men who were full of hatred. Though we may deplore and condemn such actions from a humane point of view, we still have to acknowledge their unconditional, relentless and irrevocable nature. No deals were done, there was no pretence, no concessions were made. What those revolutionaries did they did wholeheartedly, resolutely, regardless of conscience, morality or custom. Both the Jacobins and the Bolsheviks butchered the ruling upper classes and executed their royal families. They broke with Christianity and waged war on it, intending to wipe it off the face of the earth. They succeeded in involving the people of their nations in wars fought with energy and enthusiasm – the revolutionary wars of the past, the war against Germany today. Their theories and revolutionary ideas had enormous influence beyond the frontiers of their own countries.

The methods of the National Socialists are different, but basically they too pursue a single idea: the extermination and annihilation of people who think differently from them. Now and then a certain number of Germans are shot, but the fact is hushed up and kept from public knowledge. People are imprisoned in concentration camps, allowed to waste away there and perish. The public hears nothing about it. If you are going to arrest enemies of the State you should have the courage to accuse them publicly and hand them over to public justice.

On the one hand, they ally themselves with the ruling classes in capital and industry and maintain the capitalist principle, on the other they preach socialism. They declare themselves in favour of the right to personal and religious freedom, but they destroy the Christian churches and conduct a secret, underground battle against them. They speak of the *Führer* principle and the rights of capable people to develop their talents freely, but they make everything dependent on Party membership. Even the most able and brilliant are ignored if they stay outside the Party. Hitler says he is offering the world peace, but at the same time he is arming in a disturbing manner. He tells the world he has no intention of incorporating other nations into the German states and denying them the right to their own sovereignty, but what about the Czechs; what about the Poles and the Serbs? Especially in Poland, there can have been no need to rob a nation of sovereignty in its own self-contained area of settlement.

And look at the National Socialists themselves – see how far they really live by National Socialist principles: for instance, the idea that the common good comes before the individual good. They ask ordinary people to observe that principle but have no intention of doing so themselves. Who faces the enemy? The people, not the Party. Now they are calling up the physically infirm to serve in the army, while you see healthy, fit young men working in Party offices and the police, far from the firing line. Why are they exempt?

They seize Polish and Jewish property to enjoy it themselves. Now the Poles and the Jews have nothing to eat, they live in want, they are freezing, and the National Socialists see nothing wrong in taking everything for themselves.

Warsaw, 17 April 1942

I have spent a number of peaceful days here at the College of Physical Education. I hardly notice the war, but I can't feel happy. Now and then we hear of this or that. It's the events in the area behind the front lines that make the news here: the shootings, the accidents, and so on. In Lietzmannstadt [Łódź] a hundred people were killed – executed although innocent, you might say – because some bandits fired on three police officers. The same has happened in Warsaw. The result is to arouse not fear and terror but bitter determination, anger and rising fanaticism. On the Praga bridge two Hitler Youth boys were molesting a Pole, and when he defended himself they called a German policeman to their aid. Thereupon the Pole shot all three of them down. A large military car simply ran down a rickshaw containing three people in the post office square. The driver of the rickshaw was killed at once. The military car drove on, dragging the rickshaw, which still had a passenger in it, along under the vehicle. A crowd of people gathered, but still the car drove on. One German tried to stop it. Then the rickshaw became entangled in the car's wheels so that it had to stop. The men in the car came to a halt, pulled the rickshaw away and drove on.

Some of the Poles in Zakopane failed to hand in their skis. Houses were searched, and two hundred and forty men were sent to Auschwitz, the deeply feared concentration camp in the east. The G.Sta.Po torture people to death there. They drive the unfortunates into a cell and make short work of them by gassing them. People are savagely beaten during interrogation. And there are special torture cells: for instance, one where the victim's hands and arms are tied to a column which is then pulled up, and the victim hangs there until he becomes unconscious. Or he is put in a crate where he can only crouch, and left there until he loses consciousness. What other diabolical things have they devised? How many totally innocent people are held in their prisons? Food is getting scarcer every day; famine is growing in Warsaw.

Tomaszów, 26 June 1942

I hear organ music and singing from the Catholic church. I go in; children in white taking their first communion are standing at the altar. There is a crowd of people in the church. They are just singing the *Tantum ergo*, and the blessing is being given. I let the priest bless me too. Innocent little children in a Polish city here, in a German city there, or in some other country, all praying to God, and in a few years' time they will be fighting and killing each other with blind hatred. Even in the old days, when nations were more religious and called their rulers Christian majesties, it was the same as today when people are moving away from Christianity. Humanity seems doomed to do more evil than good. The greatest ideal on earth is human love.

Warsaw, 23 July 1942

If you read the newspapers and listen to the news on the radio you might think everything was going very well, peace was certain, the war already won and the future of the German people full of hope. However, I just can't believe it, if only because injustice cannot prevail in the long run, and the way the Germans rule the countries they have conquered is bound to lead to resistance sooner or later. I only have to look at conditions here in Poland, and I don't see much of them either, because we are told very little. But we can form a clear picture, all the same, from all the observations, conversations and information we hear every day. If methods of administration and government, the oppression of the local people and the operations of the G.Sta.Po are particularly brutal here, I suppose it's very much the same in the other conquered countries.

There is outright terror and fear everywhere, the use of force, arrests. People are taken away and shot daily. The life of a human being, let alone his personal freedom, is a matter of no importance. But the love of freedom is native to every human being and every nation, and cannot be suppressed in the long term. History teaches us that tyranny has never endured. And now we have blood-guilt on our conscience for the dreadful injustice of murdering the Jewish inhabitants. There is an action going on here to exterminate the Jews. That has been the aim of the German civilian administration ever since the occupation of the eastern regions, with the assistance of the police and the G.Sta.Po, but apparently it is to be applied on a huge, radical scale now.

We hear credible reports from all kinds of different sources that the ghetto in Lublin has been cleared, the Jews brought out of it and murdered *en masse*, or driven into the forests, and that some of them have been imprisoned in a camp. People from Lietzmannstadt and Kutno say that the Jews – men, women and children – are poisoned in mobile gas vehicles, the dead are stripped of their clothes, thrown into mass graves, and the clothing goes to textiles factories for reprocessing. Dreadful scenes are said to go on there. Now the reports say they are emptying the Warsaw ghetto in the same way. There are some four hundred thousand people in

it, and Ukrainian and Lithuanian police battalions are used
for the purpose instead of the German police. It is hard to
believe all this, and I try not to, not so much out of anxiety
for the future of our nation, which will have to pay for these
monstrous things some day – but because I can't believe
Hitler wants such a thing and there are Germans who will
give such orders. If it is so, there can be only one explanation:
they're sick, abnormal or mad.

25 July 1942

If what they are saying in the city is true – and it does come
from reliable sources – then it is no honour to be a German
officer, and no one could go along with what's happening.
But I can't believe it.

The rumours say that thirty thousand Jews are to be taken
from the ghetto this week and sent east somewhere. In spite
of all the secrecy, people say they know what happens then:
somewhere near Lublin, buildings have been constructed
with rooms that can be electrically heated by heavy current,
like the electricity in a crematorium. Unfortunate people are
driven into these heated rooms and burnt alive, and thousands can be killed like that in a day, saving all the trouble
of shooting them, digging mass graves and then filling them
in. The guillotine of the French Revolution can't compete,
and even in the cellars of the Russian secret police they
haven't devised such virtuoso methods of mass slaughter.

But surely this is madness. It can't be possible. You wonder
why the Jews don't defend themselves. However, many,
indeed most of them, are so weak from starvation and misery
that they couldn't offer any resistance.

Warsaw, 13 August 1942

A Polish shopkeeper expelled from Posen at the beginning of the war has a business here in Warsaw. He often sells me fruit, vegetables and so on. During the First World War he fought as a German soldier for four years, on the Western Front. He showed me his pay-book. This man sympathizes strongly with the Germans, but he is a Pole and always will be. He is in despair at the dreadful cruelties, the animal brutality of what the Germans are doing in the ghetto.

You can't help wondering again and again how there can possibly be such riff-raff among our own people. Have the criminals and lunatics been let out of the prisons and asylums and sent here to act as bloodhounds? No, it's people of some prominence in the State who have taught their otherwise harmless countrymen to act like this. Evil and brutality lurk in the human heart. If they are allowed to develop freely they flourish, putting out dreadful offshoots, the kind of ideas necessary if the Jews and the Poles are to be murdered like this.

The Polish shopkeeper I mentioned has Jewish acquaintances in the ghetto and visits it often. He says the sights there are intolerable, and he is afraid to go now. Going down the street in a rickshaw, he saw a G.Sta.Po man forcing a number of Jews, both men and women, into the doorway of a building and then shooting into the crowd at random. Ten people were killed or wounded. One man ran away, and the G.Sta.Po man aimed at him too, but the magazine of his pistol was empty. The wounded died. No one helped them; the doctors have already been taken away or killed, and anyway they were supposed to die. A woman told my Polish acquaintance that several of the G.Sta.Po made their way into the Jewish maternity hospital, took the babies away, put them in a sack, went off and threw them into a hearse. These wicked men were unmoved by the crying of the infants and their mothers' heart-rending wails. You would hardly believe it, and yet it's true. Two such animals were on a tram with me yesterday. They had whips in their hands and they were coming from the ghetto. I would have liked to push them under the tram wheels.

What cowards we are, thinking ourselves above all this, but letting it happen. We shall be punished for it too. And so will our innocent children, for we are colluding when we allow these crimes to be committed.

After 21 August 1942

Lying is the worst of all evils. Everything else that is diabolical comes from it. And we have been lied to; public opinion is constantly deceived. Not a page of a newspaper is free of lies, whether it deals with political, economic, historical, social or cultural affairs. Truth is under pressure everywhere; the facts are distorted, twisted and made into their opposite. Can this turn out well? No, things can't go on like this, for the sake of human nature and the free human spirit. The liars and those who distort the truth must perish and be deprived of their power to rule by force, and then there may be room for a freer, nobler kind of humanity again.

1 September 1942

Why did this war have to happen at all? Because humanity had to be shown where its godlessness was taking it. First of all Bolshevism killed millions, saying it was done to introduce a new world order. But the Bolshevists could act as they did only because they had turned away from God and Christian teaching. Now National Socialism is doing the same in Germany. It forbids people to practise their religion, the young are brought up godless, the Church is opposed and its property appropriated, anyone who thinks differently is terrorized, the free human nature of the German people is debased and they are turned into terrified slaves. The truth is kept from them. They can play no part in the fate of their nation.

There are no commandments now against stealing, killing or lying, not if they go against people's personal interest. This denial of God's commandments leads to all the other immoral manifestations of greed – unjust self-enrichment, hatred, deceit, sexual licence resulting in infertility and the downfall of the German people. God allows all this to happen, lets these forces have power and allows so many innocent people to perish to show mankind that without him we are only animals in conflict, who believe we have to destroy each other. We will not listen to the divine commandment: 'Love one another'. Very well, then, says God, try the Devil's commandment, the opposite: 'Hate one another'. We know the story of the Deluge from Holy Scripture. Why did the first race of men come to such a tragic end? Because they had abandoned God and must die, guilty and innocent alike. They had only themselves to blame for their punishment. And it is the same today.

6 September 1942

A Special Commando Unit officer taking part in the fencing tournament told me about the dreadful things the unit has done in the town of Sielce, an administrative centre. He was so upset and indignant that he entirely forgot we were in quite a large company including a top G.Sta.Po man. One day the Jews were driven out of the ghetto and taken through the streets: men, women and children. A number of them were shot publicly in front of the Germans and the Polish population. Women were left writhing in their blood in the summer heat, and given no help. Children who had hidden were thrown out of the windows. Then all these thousands of people were taken to a place near the railway station, where trains were supposed to be ready to take them away. They waited there for three days in the heat of summer, without food or drink. If anyone rose to his feet he was shot at once, and that was done publicly too. Then they were taken away, two hundred people crammed into a cattle truck only large enough for forty-two. What happened to them? Nobody will admit to knowing, but it can't be concealed. More and more people are managing to escape, and they make these dreadful things known. The place is called Treblinka, in the east of German-ruled Polish territory. The trucks are unloaded there; many people are already dead. The whole place is enclosed by walls, and the trucks go right in before they are unloaded. The dead are heaped up beside the railway tracks. When healthy men arrive they have to take the mountains of corpses away, dig new graves and cover them when they are full. Then they themselves are shot. Other transports come bringing men to deal with their predecessors. The thousands of women and children have to undress, and then they are taken into a mobile hut and gassed there. The hut is driven up to a pit, and a device opens up the side wall and raises the floor, tipping the corpses into their grave. This has been going for on a long time. Unfortunate people from all over Poland are being assembled. Some are killed on the spot because there isn't enough loading capacity available, but if there are too many for that they are taken away. A dreadful stench of corpses hangs over the whole Treblinka area. My confidant was told all this by a Jew who escaped. He and seven others managed to get away, and now he is living in Warsaw; I'm told there are quite a number of them in the city. He showed my acquaintance a twenty-złoty note he had taken from the pocket of a corpse; he wrapped the note up carefully so that the stench of the corpses would cling to it, as a constant reminder to him to avenge his brothers.

Sunday, 14 February 1943
On a Sunday, when you can indulge in your own thoughts and forget the army and its demands, all the ideas you usually hide in your unconscious mind come up. I feel great anxiety about the future. Then again, looking back over this wartime period, I just cannot understand how we have been able to commit such crimes against defenceless civilians, against the Jews. I ask myself again and again, how is it possible? There can be only one explanation: the people who could do it, who gave the orders and allowed it to happen, have lost all sense of decency and responsibility. They are godless through and through, gross egotists, despicable materialists. When the terrible mass murders of Jews were committed last summer, so many women and children slaughtered, I knew quite certainly that we would lose the war. There was now no point in a war that might once have been justified as a search for free subsistence and living space – it had degenerated into vast, inhuman mass slaughter, negating all cultural values, and it can never be justified to the German people; it will be utterly condemned by the nation as a whole. All the torturing of Poles under arrest, the shooting of prisoners of war and their bestial treatment – that can never be justified either.

16 June 1943

A young man came to see me this morning. I had met his
father in Obersig. He works in a field hospital here, and he
was an eyewitness of the shooting of a civilian by three German police officers. They demanded the man's papers and
found out that he was a Jew, whereupon they took him into
a doorway and shot him. They took his coat away with them
and left the body lying there.

Here is another eyewitness account, from a Jew: 'We were
in a building in the ghetto. We held out in the cellar for
seven days. The building burnt above us, the women ran out
and so did we men, and some of us were shot. Then we were
taken to the *Umschlagplatz* and loaded into cattle trucks.
My brother took poison, our wives were taken to Treblinka
and burnt there. I was sent to a labour camp. We were treated
dreadfully, got almost nothing to eat and had to work hard.'
He has written to his friends saying, 'Send me poison; I can't
endure this. So many people are dying.'

Mrs Jait worked as a domestic servant for the secret service
for a year. She often saw the terrible way they treated the
Jews who worked there. They were savagely beaten. One
Jew had to spend a whole day standing on a heap of coke
in terrible cold, without warm clothing. A secret service man
passing by just shot him down. Innumerable Jews have been
killed like that, for no reason, senselessly. It's beyond understanding.

Now the last remnants of the Jewish inhabitants of the
ghetto are being exterminated. An SS Sturmführer boasted
of the way they shot the Jews down as they ran out of the
burning buildings. The entire ghetto has been razed by fire.

These brutes think we shall win the war that way. But we
have lost the war with this appalling mass murder of the

Jews. We have brought shame upon ourselves that cannot
be wiped out; it's a curse that can't be lifted. We deserve no
mercy; we are all guilty.

I am ashamed to go into the city. Any Pole has a right to
spit at us. German soldiers are being shot daily. It will get
worse, and we have no right to complain, for we deserve
nothing else. Every day I'm here I feel worse and worse.

6 July 1943

Why does God permit this terrible war with its dreadful
human sacrifices? Think of the terrible air raids, the awful
fear of the innocent civilian population, the inhumanity of
the treatment of prisoners in the concentration camps, the
murder of hundreds of thousands of Jews by the Germans.
Is it God's fault? Why doesn't he step in, why does he let it
all happen? We might ask such questions, but we will get no
answer. We are so willing to blame others instead of ourselves. God allows evil to come about because mankind has
espoused it, and now we are beginning to feel the burden of
our own evil and imperfections. When the Nazis came to
power we did nothing to stop them; we betrayed our own
ideals. Ideals of personal, democratic and religious freedom.

The workers went along with the Nazis, the Church stood
by and watched, the middle classes were too cowardly to do
anything, and so were the leading intellectuals. We allowed
the unions to be abolished, the various religious denomi-
nations to be suppressed, there was no freedom of speech in
the press or on the radio. Finally we let ourselves be driven into
war. We were content for Germany to do without democratic
representation and put up with pseudo-representation by
people with no real say in anything. Ideals can't be betrayed
with impunity, and now we must all take the consequences.

5 December 1943

The last year has seen one setback after another. Now we
are fighting on the Dnieper. The whole of the Ukraine is
lost. Even if we retained the remnant we still have in that
area, there could surely be no question of economic gain.
The Russians are so strong that they will always drive us out
of their territory. The British offensive in Italy has begun,
and there again we are giving up position after position.
German cities are being destroyed one by one. It is Berlin's
turn now, and there have been air raids on Leipzig since
2 September. The U-boat war is a total failure. What do the
people who still speak of victory think they can expect? We
haven't been able to win over a single country that we have
occupied to our cause. Our allies, Bulgaria, Romania and
Hungary, can provide only local help. They are glad enough
if they can cope with their own internal problems, and they're
preparing for the enemy powers to attack their borders. They
can't do anything for us except through economic help – for
instance, Romanian oil deliveries. In military terms their aid
is practically worthless. Since the overthrow of the Fascist
government in Italy the country is nothing to us but a theatre
of war outside the borders of the Reich, where fighting is
still going on, for the moment.

The superior force of our enemies knocks the weapons
from our hands. Anyone who tries standing upright is felled.
That's the present state of things, so how can we think we
might yet make the war turn out in our favour?

No one in Germany believes we will win the war any more
either, but what way out is there? There'll be no revolution
at home because no one has the courage to risk his life by
standing up to the G.Sta.Po. And what use would it be if a
few did try? The majority of people might agree with them,

but the majority is fettered. There's been no chance for the last ten years for individuals, far less the population at large, to express free will. G.Sta.Po bullets would start flying at once. And we can't expect an army coup. The army is willingly being driven to its death, and any idea of opposition that might set off a mass movement is quickly suppressed there too. So we must go on to the bitter end. Our entire nation will have to pay for all these wrongs and this unhappiness, all the crimes we have committed. Many innocent people must be sacrificed before the blood-guilt we've incurred can be wiped out. That's an inexorable law in small and large things alike.

1 January 1944

The German newspapers are indignantly reporting the confiscation and removal of art treasures by the Americans in the south of Italy. Such an outcry over other people's crimes is truly ludicrous – as if the enemy didn't know about the art treasures we've appropriated and exported from Poland, or those we have destroyed in Russia.

Even if we adopt the 'my country right or wrong' view and accept what we have done with equanimity, such hypocrisy is out of place and can only make us look ridiculous.

11 August 1944

The Führer is to issue a decree that Warsaw is to be razed to the ground. A start has been made already. All the streets liberated in the uprising are being destroyed by fire. The inhabitants have to leave the city, and are going westward in crowds of many thousands. If the news of this decree is true then it's clear to me that we have lost Warsaw, and with it Poland and the war itself. We are giving up a place we held for five years, extending it and telling the world it was a forfeit of war. Monstrous methods were used here. We acted as if we were the masters and would never go away. Now we can't help seeing that all is lost, we're destroying our own work, everything of which the civil administration was so proud – it saw its great cultural tasks as being here and wanted to prove their necessity to the world. Our policy in the east is bankrupt, and we are erecting a final memorial to it with the destruction of Warsaw.

Epilogue

A Bridge Between
Władysław Szpilman and
Wilm Hosenfeld

Wolf Biermann

Wolf Biermann is one of Germany's best-known poets, song-writers and essayists. He was born in Hamburg in 1936, the son of a communist family. His father, a Jewish shipyard worker and a resistance fighter, was murdered in Auschwitz in 1943. As a teenager, Biermann went east, against the stream of refugees going the other way to West Germany. In 1965 his works were banned in East Germany because of their attacks on the government, and in 1976 Biermann was forced by the authorities to emigrate to West Germany. He now lives in Hamburg.

This book needs neither a foreword nor an afterword, and indeed it does not really require any commentary. However, the author, Władysław Szpilman, asked me to provide some annotations for his readers – half a century after the events he describes.

He wrote his story, as it is printed here, in Warsaw directly after the war, that is to say in the heat of the moment, or more accurately in deep shock. There are many books in which people have set down their memories of the Shoah. Most accounts of survival, however, were not written until some years or decades after the events they describe. I imagine that several obvious reasons will spring to mind.

Readers will notice that although this book was written amidst the still smouldering ashes of the Second World War, its language is surprisingly cool. Władysław Szpilman describes his recent sufferings with an almost melancholy detachment. It seems to me as if he had not really come back to his senses yet after his journey through all the various circles of the inferno; as if he were writing in some surprise about another person, the person he became after the German invasion of Poland.

His book was first published in Poland in 1946 under the title of one of its chapters, *Death of a City*. It was very soon withdrawn from circulation by Stalin's Polish minions, and has not been reissued since, either in Poland or outside. As the countries conquered by the Red Army gradually became more firmly caught in the stranglehold of their liberators, the *nomenklatura* of Eastern Europe in general were unable to tolerate such authentic eyewitness accounts as this book.

They contained too many painful truths about the collabor-
ation of defeated Russians, Poles, Ukrainians, Latvians and
Jews with the German Nazis.

Even in Israel, people did not want to hear about such
things. That may sound odd, but it is understandable: the
subject was intolerable to all concerned, victims and perpetrators alike, although obviously for opposite reasons.

~

> He who counted our hours
> counts on.
> What is he counting, tell me?
> He counts and counts . . .
>   (*Paul Celan*)

Numbers. More numbers. Of all the three and a half million
Jews who once lived in Poland, two hundred and forty thousand survived the Nazi period. Anti-Semitism was flourishing
long before the German invasion. Yet some three to four
hundred thousand Poles risked their lives to save Jews. Of
the sixteen thousand Aryans remembered in Yad Vashem,
the central Jewish place of remembrance in Jerusalem, one-
third were Polish. Why work it out so accurately? Because
everyone knows how horribly the infection of anti-Semitism
traditionally raged among 'the Poles', but few know that at
the same time no other nation hid so many Jews from the
Nazis. If you hid a Jew in France, the penalty was prison or
a concentration camp, in Germany it cost you your life – but
in Poland it cost the lives of your entire family.

One thing strikes me: Szpilman's emotional register seems
to include no desire for revenge. We once had a conversation
in Warsaw; he had toured the world as a pianist and was
now sitting, exhausted, at his old grand piano, which needed

tuning. He made an almost childish remark, half ironically but half in deadly earnest. 'When I was a young man I studied music for two years in Berlin. I just can't make the Germans out ... they were so extremely musical!'

This book paints a picture of life in the Warsaw ghetto on a broad canvas. Władysław Szpilman describes it in such a way that we can get a deeper understanding of something we already suspected: prisons, ghettos and concentration camps, with their huts and watchtowers and gas chambers, are not designed to ennoble the character. Hunger does not bestow an inner radiance. To put it bluntly: a scoundrel will still be a scoundrel behind barbed wire. But such a simple approach did not always apply. Certain low-life crooks and many admitted rogues behaved more bravely and helpfully in the ghetto or the concentration camp than a good many educated, respectable middle-class people.

At times Władysław Szpilman describes the Shoah in plain prose as densely written as poetry. I think of the scene at the *Umschlagplatz*, when Szpilman was already doomed to destruction, selected for transport to an uncertain future which everyone suspected would be certain death. The author, his parents and his brother and sisters share a cream caramel cut into six, their last meal together. And I recall the dentist's impatience as they waited for the death train: 'It's a disgrace to us all! We're letting them take us to our death like sheep to the slaughter! If we attacked the Germans, half a million of us, we could break out of the ghetto, or at least die honourably, not as a stain on the face of history!'; and the response given by Szpilman's father: 'Look, we're not heroes! We're perfectly ordinary people, which is why we prefer to risk hoping for that ten per cent chance of living.' As can happen in a genuine tragedy, both the dentist and Szpilman's father were right. Jews have argued this unanswerable question of resistance among themselves thousands of times, over and over again, and they will be doing so for generations to come. A more practical consideration occurs to me: how could these people, all civilians, how could women and children and old folk abandoned by God and the world, how could starved, sick men in fact have defended themselves against such a perfect extermination machine?

Resistance was impossible, but all the same there *was* Jewish resistance. The armed fighting in the Warsaw ghetto and thousands of brave deeds performed by Jewish partisans show that it was a very capable resistance too. There were the risings in Sobibór and even in Treblinka. I think also of Lydia Vago and Sarah Ehrenhalt in Israel, who survived as slaves in the Union ammunition factory in Auschwitz, where the explosives to blow up one of the crematoria came from.

Władysław Szpilman's story shows that he played a direct part in the brave resistance. He was among those who were taken out daily in labour columns to the Aryan side of the city, and smuggled not just bread and potatoes but ammunition for the Jewish resistance back into the ghetto. He mentions this brave deed modestly and only in passing.

The appendix publishes, for the first time, entries from the diary of Wilm Hosenfeld, a Wehrmacht officer without whom Szpilman, a Polish Jew, would probably not have survived at all. Hosenfeld, a teacher, had already served as a lieutenant in the First World War, and may therefore have been considered too old for service in the front line at the beginning of the Second. That could have been the reason why he was made officer in charge of all the Warsaw sports facilities taken over by the Wehrmacht so that German soldiers could keep fit there with games and athletics. Captain Hosenfeld was taken prisoner by the Soviet army in the final days of the war, and died in captivity seven years later.

At the beginning of the tale of Szpilman's wanderings, one of the hated Jewish police saved him. At the end it was Captain Hosenfeld who found the half-dead pianist in the ruined city of Warsaw, now empty of its inhabitants – and did not kill him. Hosenfeld even brought food, an eiderdown and an overcoat to the Jew's hiding place. This is like some Hollywood fairy-tale, yet it is true: one of the hated master race played the part of guardian angel in this dreadful story. Since Hitler's Germany had obviously lost the war anyway, the fugitive, with forethought, gave his anonymous helper a useful piece of information. 'If anything happens to you, if I can help you then in any way, remember my name: Szpilman, Polish Radio.' I know from Szpilman that he began looking for his saviour at once in 1945 – unsuccessfully. When he went to the place where his violinist friend had seen the man, the camp had been moved.

Hosenfeld finally died in a prisoner of war camp at Stalingrad, a year before Stalin's death. He had been tortured in captivity because the Soviet officers thought his claim to have saved a Jew a particularly outrageous lie. He then suffered several cerebral strokes. By the end he was in a confused state of mind, a beaten child who does not understand the blows. He died with his spirit utterly broken.

Hosenfeld just managed to send his diaries to Germany. His last home leave was at Whitsun 1944; there is an attractive picture of the officer home from the dirty war, wearing his bright white uniform, with his wife and his beloved children around him. It looks like an idyll of eternal peace. The

Hosenfeld family kept the two densely written notebooks containing the diary. The last entry bears the date 11 August 1944, which means that Hosenfeld sent his most explosive comments by the ordinary army post. Suppose those two volumes had fallen into the hands of the dreaded gentlemen in leather coats . . . it hardly bears thinking of. They would have taken the man apart.

Hosenfeld's son gave me an account which provides a vivid picture of his dead father:

'My father was an enthusiastic, warm-hearted teacher. In the period after the First World War, when beating children was still the usual means of discipline in schools, his kindness to his pupils was very unconventional. He used to take the children in the youngest class of the Spessart village school on his knee if they were having difficulty with the alphabet. And he always had two handkerchiefs in his trouser pocket, one for himself and one for his youngest pupils' snotty noses.

'In the winter of 1939 to 1940 my father's unit, which had left Fulda for Poland in the autumn of 1939, was stationed in the little town of Wegrow, east of Warsaw. Earlier on the German commissariat had appropriated supplies of hay there which belonged to the Polish army. One cold winter's day my father happened to come by as an SS man was taking a schoolboy away. The boy had been caught stealing some of the requisitioned hay in a barn, probably just an armful. Obviously the child was about to be shot as a punishment for his offence and to deter others.

'My father told me he rushed at the SS man shouting, "You can't kill that child!" The SS man drew his pistol, pointed it at my father and said menacingly, "If you don't get out at once we'll kill you too!"

'It took my father a long time to recover from this experience. He spoke of it just once, two or three years later when he was on leave. I was the only member of the family to hear the story.'

~

Władysław Szpilman began working for Radio Warsaw again as a pianist at once. He opened the broadcasting service after the war with the same Chopin piece he had been playing live on the radio that last day, amidst a hail of German artillery and bombs. You could say that the broadcast of Chopin's Nocturne in C sharp minor was only interrupted, briefly, so that in the six-year interval Herr Hitler could play his part on the world stage.

Władysław Szpilman heard no more of his rescuer until the year 1949. In 1950, however, there was a further development. A Polish Jew, one Leon Warm, emigrated from Poland and visited the Hosenfelds in West Germany on the way. One of Wilm Hosenfeld's sons writes, of Leon Warm:

'In the first few years after the war my mother was living with my younger brother and sister in part of our former accommodation at the school in Thalau, a little village in the Rhön region. On 14 November 1950 a pleasant young Pole turned up and asked for my father, whom he had met in Warsaw during the war.

'On the way to the extermination camp of Treblinka, this man had managed to open a hatch closed with barbed wire in the cattle truck where he and his companions in misfortune were locked. Then he jumped out of the moving train. Through a family he knew in Warsaw he met our father, who got him a pass with a false name and took him on as a worker at the sports centre. Since then he had been working as a chemist in Poland, and now he intended to start a firm of his own in Australia.'

This man, Leon Warm, learned from his visit to Frau Hosenfeld that her husband was still alive. She had received some letters and cards. Frau Hosenfeld even showed him a list of Jews and Poles whom her husband had saved, on a postcard dated 15 July 1946. He had asked his wife to go to these people for help. Number four on the list could be deciphered as 'Wladislaus Spielmann, pianist with Warsaw Radio'.

Three members of a family called Cieciora had a Hosenfeld story of their own to tell. The first days of the German blitzkrieg saw the following scene take place: the wife of a Pole called Stanisław Cieciora went to a prisoner of war camp in Pabianice where she had been told her wounded husband, a soldier in the defeated army, was being held; he must have been afraid he would be killed by the victors. On her way she met a German officer riding a bicycle. He asked where she was going. Paralysed by fear, she stammered out the truth. 'My husband's a soldier – he's sick in the camp there, I'm soon going to have our child, and I'm frightened for him.' The German wrote down the man's name and sent his wife back, promising her, 'Your husband will be home again in three days' time.' And so he was.

After that, Hosenfeld visited the Cieciora family on occasion and they made friends. This extraordinary German began learning Polish. Being a devout Catholic, Hosenfeld even sometimes went to church with his new friends, wearing his Wehrmacht uniform and attending the ordinary Polish service. What a picture: a German, very correct in the 'coat of the murderers', kneeling before a Polish priest, while the 'subhuman Slav' laid the wafer representing the body of Christ on a German tongue.

One thing led to another: the Cieciora family were anxious about the husband's brother, a priest in the political underground wanted by the Germans. Hosenfeld saved him too. Thirdly, he saved a relation of the Ciecioras by rescuing him from an army truck. I found out how both rescues happened in an account by Captain Hosenfeld's daughter:

'In the spring of 1973 we had a visit from Maciej Cieciora of Posen [Poznań]. His uncle, a Catholic priest, had to flee from the Gestapo after the German invasion in the autumn of 1939. My father, who was then officer in charge of the sporting facilities of the city of Warsaw appropriated by the Wehrmacht, protected him by giving him work at his office under the false name of "Cichocki". It was through Father Cieciora, with whom he soon became close friends, that my father met the priest's brother-in-law Koschel.

'Maciej Cieciora told us that, probably in 1943, Polish freedom fighters had shot some German soldiers in the part of Warsaw where the Koschel family lived. Thereupon an SS unit in that quarter arrested a number of men – including Mr Koschel – and loaded them up on a truck. The unfortunate men were to be executed immediately outside the city in reprisal.

'As chance would have it my father met this truck at a road junction when he was walking through the city centre. Mr Koschel recognized an officer he knew on the pavement and waved to him vigorously and desperately. My father took in the situation at once, and with great presence of mind stepped into the road and gestured to the driver to stop. The driver came to a halt. "I need a man!" my father said in commanding tones to the SS leader in charge. He went up to the truck, inspected the occupants, and picked out Koschel as if at random. They let him out, and so he was saved.'

It's a small world. Today, in the eighth year after the collapse of the Eastern bloc, Stanisław Cieciora's son is the Polish consul in Hamburg. He told me a moving little story: his grateful parents in Samter-Karolin sent the fatherless Hosenfeld family food-parcels of sausage and butter, from starving Poland to Hitler's Germany, even during the war itself. It's a strange world too.

~

Leon Warm got in touch with Szpilman in Warsaw, care of Polish Radio, conveying to him the names of the people Hosenfeld had saved and passing on his urgent request for help. That was nearly half a century ago.

In 1957 Władysław Szpilman toured West Germany with the brilliant violinist Gimpel. The two musicians visited Wilm Hosenfeld's family in Thalau: his wife Annemarie and his two sons Helmut and Detlef. Their mother gave her visitor a photograph of her husband. It is printed in this book. Last summer, when it was decided that this almost forgotten book was to be reissued in German, I asked the old man about the background of the Hosenfeld story.

'You know, I don't like to talk about it. I've never discussed it with anyone, not even my wife and my two sons. Why not, you ask? Because I was ashamed. You see, when I finally found out the German officer's name at the end of 1950 I wrestled with my fears and overcame my distaste, and I went as a humble petitioner to a criminal whom no decent person in Poland would speak to: one Jakub Berman.

'Berman was the most powerful man in Poland, head of the Polish NKWD, and a bastard, as everyone knew. He was more influential than the minister of the interior. But I was determined to try, so I went to see him and told him everything, adding that I wasn't the only one Hosenfeld had saved: he had saved Jewish children too, and he bought shoes for Polish children at the very beginning of the war and gave them food. I also told him about Leon Warm and the Cieciora family, emphasizing the fact that a great many people owed their lives to this German. Berman was friendly, and promised to do something. After a few days he even called at our home in person: he was sorry, but there was nothing to be done. "If your German were still in Poland, then we could get him out," he said. "But our comrades in the Soviet Union won't let him go. They say your officer belonged to a detachment that was involved in spying – so there's nothing we can do about it as Poles, and I'm powerless," he concluded – a man who was all-powerful by the grace of Stalin. So I approached the worst rogue of the lot, and it did no good.'

Directly after the war it was impossible to publish a book in Poland which presented a German officer as a brave and helpful man. It may interest readers to know that for the Polish edition Władysław Szpilman found himself obliged to pretend that his rescuer Wilm Hosenfeld was an Austrian. An Austrian angel was obviously 'not quite so bad' at the time, absurd as it seems today. In the years of the Cold War Austria and East Germany were linked by a common piece of hypocrisy: both pretended to have been forcibly occupied by Hitler's Germany in the Second World War.

~

In Yad Vashem there is an Avenue of the Just where young
trees have been planted, one for every Gentile who saved
Jews from the Holocaust. Small plates on the young trees
growing in the stony soil bear the names of these brave
people. Anyone going to the great museum passes thousands
of such names. I hope to ensure that there is soon a tree
growing for Captain Wilm Hosenfeld in the Avenue of the
Just, watered by the river Jordan. As for who will plant it –
who but Władysław Szpilman, with the support of his son
Andrzej?